CASH
UNCOMPLICATED

Please note that much of this publication is based on personal experience and anecdotal evidence. Although the author has made every reasonable attempt to achieve complete accuracy of the content of this book, he makes no representations or warranties with respect to the accuracy or completeness of the contents of this book and specifically disclaims any implied warranties for a particular purpose. Your particular circumstances may not be suited to the examples described in the book. You should use information in this book at your own risk. Nothing in this book is intended to replace common sense or legal, accounting, or professional advice, and is meant only to inform.

Isla Vista Press

1267 Willis St, Ste 200

Redding, CA, 96001

ISBN: 978-1-7359381-0-3 (print)

ISBN: 978-1-7359381-1-0(ebook)

Ordering Information:

Special discounts are available on quantity purchases by corporations, associations, and others. For details, contact aaron@cashuncomplicated.com

This book is dedicated to my family. Thank you to my parents and sister for always believing in me. To my wife, Jennifer, thank you for your encouragement and for pushing me to keep improving. To my two girls, this book is written for you. I love you all very much!

TABLE OF CONTENTS

CASH UNCOMPLICATED

A NEW MINDSET TO BUILDING WEALTH

AARON NANNINI

Introduction

I never thought I would be successful with my personal finances, much less be in a position to write a book about them. The subject was as foreign to me as traveling to Mars. My personal finances used to mean how much money I would have each month to pay rent, spend at bars, and take a trip now and then.

"Saving" used to mean accumulating just enough money either to buy something or go on a trip. Not surprisingly, my bank account usually only had hundreds of dollars in it—closer to zero than a thousand. I was the classic paycheck to paycheck story. One missed paycheck and I would have been in financial trouble. As I entered my early thirties, my finances weren't any better. I made excuse after excuse. Learning to save and invest my money almost happened by accident.

During the Great Recession, home prices got so low where I live in Southern California, they were impossible to ignore. I didn't know much about real estate at the time, but I knew it was less expensive to own than to rent so I decided to buy. As an educator in the local school district, I didn't make enough money to buy a house, but I was able to scrape together just enough to purchase a one bedroom condo. It wasn't much but it was mine, and I took pride in owning it.

I thought I'd live in my one bedroom condo for at least 10 years. I continued to live paycheck to paycheck and just got by. I made the mortgage payments but wasn't financially comfortable. Just opening my credit card or bank statement made my heart race; I always held my breath in hopes that I had more in my checking account than what I owed on the credit card. I basically broke even every month and gained little equity on my one bedroom condo.

A few years later, my then girlfriend, now wife, moved in with me. I spent fewer nights out, and with two incomes, we suddenly had a surplus each month. My first instinct was still to find ways to spend it or to go on extra trips. But then it occurred to me we might try to buy a house. The housing market was finally starting to recover from the economic downturn, and it seemed like a good time to buy. We both felt that if we didn't buy soon, we were going to get priced out of the expensive Southern California market and would be living in the condo for many years to come.

With our wedding only a few months away, we purchased a small, three bedroom house. It was barely over 1,000 square feet but it was home. We still had almost no equity in the condo so we decided to keep it as a rental.

That good decision to buy a home led to other good decisions, and eventually led to me educating myself about personal finance. During my journey, I have learned that the real purpose of saving money is to use that money to invest and grow. Saving should be purposeful, planned out, and intentional. This is contrary to what advertisements tell us and what friends tell us about their lives on Facebook and Instagram. The messages there are to spend, spend, spend, and life will be great.

What I have learned, and continue to learn, is that when I prioritize my values and align my personal finances with my values, my life becomes much more satisfying than any temporary high I might get from spending money. Being highly intentional with money and saving to invest has given me power and control over my personal finances that I never thought possible. The daily pressure and fear of living paycheck to paycheck is long gone.

Four years ago, my wife and I welcomed our first daughter. Three years later, we welcomed girl number two. They are the biggest reasons why I wrote this book. I want my two girls to understand money and never feel controlled or powerless by it like I did.

I want them to invest and never be in the paycheck to paycheck rut that I was in for too many years. I want them to have their financial situations under control so that they can relax and focus on more important things like their families, friends, and passions. I want them to understand compound interest and earn it, rather than pay it. For most of my life, money was a source of fear, stress, and frustration. It is important to me that my daughters have a different experience with money. It wasn't necessary for me to struggle with money; it was a result of my lack of education, ignorance, and an unwillingness to learn. My hope is that this book will give my daughters, and many others, the tools and education to understand money.

This is a personal finance book about mindset, values, and financial behaviors. It is not designed to provide specific investment advice, though there are investment examples to show the power that smart investments can add to your life. I am not a financial advisor, nor do I pretend to be one. I am simply someone who has found financial success by following the principles and strategies outlined in this book. I am living proof that you don't need to have the salary of a doctor, lawyer, or famous athlete to attain financial success. It's not about how much you make, it's about how much you keep.

This book is not meant to replace the work you would do with a fiduciary financial advisor. Rather, this is a book that will put you in a position so that you can begin to work with one, or make investments on your own.

In order to benefit from specific financial advice, you really need to have some money first. Compound interest does not compound if you don't have any money. It seems like common sense, but far too many people put the cart before the horse. The information and principles in this book will give you the tools to start accumulating money to invest. Through common sense and easy to learn principles, you will begin to establish habits and routines that will help you generate wealth, rather than wading through financial quicksand month after month, like I did for so long.

The first focus of this book is on life goals, which will help you create financial clarity. It is critical to have crystal clear life goals, because these will dictate your financial choices and values. The second focus of the book is to show you how you can implement habits and routines into your daily life that will allow you to live by your values. The idea is to create an unyielding foundation, that once created, will support your financial success for the rest of your life.

The third focus is to explore the concept of being aware of and intentional with your money. Many of us are all too often unaware of where our money goes. We mindlessly spend it thinking that that's just how things are supposed to be. I am here to tell you it's not. This book is about being focused and intentional with your money so that you can maximize your financial potential. Being aware and intentional are cornerstone habits that are crucial to your financial success.

This book contains financial principles that are easy to understand and implement. Much of what I discuss are ideas and concepts that are so simple you will wonder why you haven't been practicing them for years. You might even have had some of these ideas yourself. Nothing in this book is complicated or difficult to implement. It contains basic, common sense principles, that when applied, will result in financial clarity and increased wealth over the years.

Each chapter concludes with simple actions you can take to immediately begin progressing toward your financial goals. Some exercises include a template so you can write out your actions in the book. Other exercises ask you to either think about certain ideas or write them down. They are all simple and easy to do.

I hope this book makes a positive impact in your life. My goal is for everyone to have a high level of financial clarity so that you can focus on the important things in life without being bogged down by financial worries. Please reach out to me on my website cashuncomplicated.com with your personal finance stories—I love hearing them!

CHAPTER 1

Mindset and Values

Whether you think you can or you can't, you're right.
– Henry Ford

Values are like fingerprints. Nobody's are the same, but you leave 'em all over everything you do.
– Elvis Presley

When I was 25, my mindset was completely backward. I wrongfully assumed that I'd never be able to afford a house and that I would buy a small condo or rent for the rest of my life. Most of my money was spent going out or on things I really didn't need. I even bought a used luxury car that ended up costing me more in repairs than any car I had ever owned or have owned since. I was ignorant and confused about money, and the scary part was I didn't understand just how confused I was.

I needed education and a change in my mindset. Just as I wrongfully assumed I'd never be able to afford a home, many Americans wrongfully assume that they will never have any success with money. This assumption creates a dangerous paradigm in which people live paycheck to paycheck, struggle to make car payments, pay just the minimum on credit card balances, and hope they can just get to the end of the month with a few bucks in their pockets. Why do we have these struggles? The answer is relatively simple: because we somehow grew to believe this is normal and what we should be doing.

Changing the norm requires thought, effort, and a resistance to what we have previously been taught about money. This shift in mindset presents an enormous challenge, because it requires undoing years of bad habits and thoughts. Some examples of my own faulty thinking included:

- "I'm broke because I'm in the education field, and I just don't make enough money."
- "California is too expensive; I'll never be able to afford a house here."
- "I can 'afford' a $450 car payment, so I'm going to just finance it."
- "I majored in a liberal arts subject in college, so I'm not supposed to be good with money."
- "I work hard, so I'm going to spend my money as it comes in and enjoy it."

You Can Be Good with Money

Money and personal finance are just like anything else in life; to be good at it, you have to practice and study. A huge component of learning to be better with money is telling yourself that you *can* be good with money.

You need to give yourself the opportunity to be good with money, which means learning, making mistakes, and having a mindset in which you grow your knowledge. Erase your old thoughts about money and get rid of the bad habits that are accepted by society as normal. Have an open mind that you can, and will, improve in this area. While having money is not the most important thing in life, understanding and learning to exert control over money will give you significant power. You either learn to control money or it controls you.

Controlling money requires an honest assessment of your values and goals. What is really important in your life? Is it having the house on the hill with a luxury car in the driveway or having more time with your family? Or do you want both? There is no right or wrong answer, but it's important to know what you want so you can create your own personal financial goals. To develop your financial goals you need to know what you want to do with your money. Tirelessly working and grinding for the sole purpose of making money is likely to leave you empty and unsatisfied. Just getting by month to month without having anything to show for it will leave you frustrated and resentful of the time you spend working. Conversely, working toward financial goals that align with your values will leave you energized, purposeful, and intentional.

The Wealthy Aren't Who You Think They Are

There is a stereotype that wealthy people were born with silver spoons in their mouths—that they're trust fund babies, inherited all their money, got lucky somehow, and didn't earn their money. This is a self-defeating mindset and a false pretense. False thinking like this tells us that we cannot become wealthy because we didn't come from a place of privilege. Consider these facts about millionaires from a survey conducted by Thomas Stanley and Sarah Fallaw in their book *The Next Millionaire Next Door*:[1]

- The vast majority of millionaires surveyed did not inherit their wealth.
- 57 percent of those surveyed reported they have always been frugal.
- The median price of a watch among millionaires surveyed is $300, and only 25 percent spent more than $25 for a pair of jeans.
- The most popular brands of cars: Toyota, Honda, and Ford. Almost 30 percent surveyed reported owning their car six years or more.
- 55 percent of surveyed millionaires graduated from a public university, 30 percent graduated from a private university.

The data shows that the stereotypes are simply wrong, and that millionaires and the wealthy are not who we think they are. It is convenient to have the mindset that the wealthy only got that way through luck or birthright. It makes us feel better to assume they didn't earn their money because it takes us off the hook and diminishes our responsibility. The problem with that mindset is that it takes away our power. The principles outlined in this book will give you tools so you can start making intelligent money decisions.

The first step is to stop thinking that financial success is a pie in the sky concept that is only attainable for people of privilege. Don't diminish your power by thinking small like this; instead move your mindset to a place of control. Start to believe that with a little bit of knowledge

---

1 Thomas J. Stanley and Sarah Stanley Fallaw, The Next Millionaire Next Door (Lanham: Lyons Press), 2019.

and application you too, can gain control of your finances and achieve extraordinary results.

Money Can't Buy Happiness, but It Sure Makes Things Easier

I can't tell you how many times I've heard people say that money can't buy happiness. I agree with the saying, but I often find myself disagreeing with the intended meaning behind it. Many of the people I've heard say this are in financial ruin. They have massive credit card debt, two car payments, student loans, and retail debt. They are drowning. They live paycheck to paycheck just to pay the minimum on their numerous bills. Many of these people are miserable and stressed out of their minds. These are not the people we should be listening to.

The saying, "Money can't buy happiness" is an excuse. It's a way to make people feel better for their financial failures and devalue an important part of their life that is causing great stress and hardship. I agree that money can't buy happiness, but getting control of your personal finances sure makes things easier. It's important to change your mindset and acknowledge that personal finances are an important part of your life that you have power and control over. You need to acknowledge that having out of control finances causes great personal stress, relationship stress, and feelings of hopelessness about the future. Once you've acknowledged this, you can work to take action and face the challenges head on.

I would like to hear more people say, "Money can't buy happiness, but it's an important aspect of life that needs to be under control" and "My money situation is under control and I have a plan to keep it that way." It would mean that they are at peace with their financial situation and that they work with their significant other to maintain a positive financial position. Money problems and ensuing arguments are one of the leading causes of divorce in the United States and other countries. How great would it be to eliminate that specific stressor so that more couples could live in harmony with each other? There is plenty to fight about in a relationship so at least eliminate money as one of those things.

Yes, keep the mindset that money can't buy happiness. That is absolutely true. The endless pursuit of money just to acquire more money is not healthy and is very unlikely to ever make us happy. However, gaining control of your personal finances makes life a lot easier and eliminates one of the biggest stressors out there.

While we all agree that money can't buy happiness, think about what money can buy. It's all about freedom and choices. Money gives us the ability to choose things and experiences based on our values, rather than being constrained by an empty bank account. It gives us the freedom to live where we want, where and how often to go on vacation, where to work, where to send the kids to school, among endless other things. The more choices we have in life, the more we can pursue what we really value.

Think of this example: What if someone had a job they hated, fought traffic every day, and worked for a boss they couldn't stand? If this person was in control of their personal finances, they wouldn't have to keep that job. While it doesn't solve all of life's problems, having money and the freedoms it affords certainly helps in a situation like that.

Abundance Mindset

The shift to an abundance mindset is one of the most important shifts you can make in your life. It opens up new doors and creates opportunities you never knew existed. The abundance mindset gives your mind permission to strive for more and not settle for less. It trains your mind to better your current situation. How does this relate to personal finance? Once you tell your mind that you can get control of your personal finances and that you deserve more than living paycheck to paycheck, or being in chronic consumer debt, you will start to believe it. Once you start to believe it, you will take action.

Saving, investing, and spending money on what you truly value creates abundance. A critical element of the abundance mindset is focus. If you have focus and vision on what is important, you can dedicate your energy and resources toward the people and things that matter most. Everything else is just noise and distraction that moves you away from your goals. The more you focus on what matters, the more you will work to achieve it.

A scarcity mindset, on the other hand, involves fear and a lack of focus. Those with a scarcity mindset are often so focused on not having enough that they forget to focus on the important things. Too often the thought process revolves around a fear of losing resources, not having enough resources, or things that are out of our control, like the weather or world politics. This fear leads to an unfocused mind, making it very difficult for people to reach their full potential. The mind is too busy looking for things that could go wrong to be fully productive. This is a very dangerous and limiting mindset that needs to be avoided at all costs.

The scarcity mindset also promotes the thought that there is not enough to go around or that you have to take from someone else to get what you want. It robs people of the opportunity to learn and work with others. This attitude holds too many people back in their financial journey and life in general.

Watch as Your Finances Grow

As you train your mind to have an abundance mindset, your personal finances will grow like you never could have imagined. Your mind will train itself to look for financial opportunities that will take your personal finances to new heights. The more you grow your money, the easier it becomes. Your mind will feed off the positive reinforcement and keep improving. It becomes a wonderful cycle of abundance and prosperity. Napoleon Hill writes in his book, *Think and Grow Rich*, "When riches begin to come, they come so quickly, in such great abundance, that one wonders where they have been hiding during all those lean years."

Money is an infinite resource to those living with an abundance mindset. There is plenty of money to be earned and acquired to create a life of abundance. There are many ways to earn and acquire money, it is up to you to create and develop new methods.

Action Item: Values and Life Goals

The process of digging deep in search of your values and life goals is an awakening process. It requires deep introspection and challenging old ideas you used to hold as absolute truth. It may be tempting to skip this step because it's difficult and uncomfortable, but don't be discouraged because working through these answers will give you clarity and focus. Your financial journey will be much easier once you pull these answers from yourself. You will also be able to relax, knowing that you did your best to create a plan and end goal. Use the template below to list your highest values. It doesn't matter what your values are, the important thing is that they are *your values*. As an example, and to give you a little background on myself, I listed my highest values in the second chart below.

Highest Life Values

Highest Value #1	
Highest Value #2	
Highest Value #3	
Highest Value #4	
Highest Value #5	

Highest Life Values (Example)

Highest Value #1	Positive relationships with family and friends—spending lots of time with and being fully engaged
Highest Value #2	Consistent exercise and healthy eating
Highest Value #3	Personal and professional growth—keep learning, keep improving, make a difference, help others
Highest Value #4	Stable finances with strong investments, strong financial reserves, value based spending—all without consumer debt
Highest Value #5	Travel, recreation

What are your highest rated values? Did you rate family highest? Health? Faith? Personal growth? What made the top five? Are you currently living your life to your highest rated values? How do your spending habits align with your values? In this exercise, many people find that their spending is out of alignment with their values. If that is the case for you, then some changes are in your future to align your values with your spending.

After completing this exercise, you should have much greater clarity about your values. This clarity directly relates to your spending habits. For example, if you rated family, faith, health, security, and personal well-being as your top five values, you probably don't want to be purchasing a new pair of shoes every month from a designer store. However, if fashion and looking good is in your top five values, a new pair of shoes every month may be in line with your values. To reiterate, writing down your values will provide you with clarity. The key is to then align your spending with your values. The remaining chapters will help you do that.

CHAPTER 2

It's Not About Deprivation: Frugality and Value-Based Spending

Don't tell me where your priorities are. Show me where you spend your money and I'll tell you what they are.
– James Frick

Frugality is a mindset of being intentional with your money and building financial systems that are consistent with your life values. It is not about penny-pinching just to save a buck and missing out on life opportunities. It's an open and honest assessment of your values and how you want to distribute your money. Frugality is about digging deep and finding your true values, then using money as a tool to move toward those values. It is also a commonsense approach to money that will give you clarity and guidance on how to control your personal finances.

Frugality is a tool to help you enjoy your hard-earned money. It naturally requires that you assess your values and follow through with consistent implementation. Frugality is a lifestyle that requires you to give thought about your wants and needs. It runs counter to the "keeping up with the Joneses" and "put everything on credit, worry about it later" mentalities that are so prevalent in our culture. A great number of principles written about in this book are based on frugality.

The word frugal is commonly misinterpreted. Being frugal is not about being cheap. Frugality really falls under the concept of *value-based spending*.

That entails determining your needs, wants, and values, and basing your spending off that. For example, if you are someone who loves sports, like I do, spending money on good seats at a football game a few times a year falls well within the range of value-based spending. If spending the money aligns with your values and you have the money, it's a good purchase and there's nothing to worry about.

Frugality and value-based spending requires going against the grain. In our consumer society, the message is to spend. But frugality requires being intentional with your money and not spending simply because everyone else is doing it. At times, this may be slightly uncomfortable if your values don't align with the people you are with. For example, if you have a group of friends who loves to go out every weekend and spend $300 on dinner and drinks when you're just as happy, or happier, to have a nice home cooked meal, that is going to be out of line with your values. You may come to a place where you suggest other places to go or hang out with these friends less. Or maybe just go out with them a couple times a year to stay in touch.

The Value Funnel and Spending Assessment Model

Buying new things gives you a temporary high and then it goes away. Whether it's a new car, a new house, or a new pair of shoes, the enjoyment is temporary. Actually, it starts even before the purchase. At the very moment you consider purchasing something, your brain gives you an increase of dopamine, creating a sense of pleasure. That's why it is so hard to resist impulse shopping—your brain is rewarding you with an increase in dopamine for even *considering* the purchase. Then you get rewarded again for making the purchase. Unfortunately, the high doesn't last long. For smaller purchases, like shoes or a handbag, the high will last a much shorter time than for big purchases like a house or car. So how do we fight against biology and the natural rewards our brain is giving us for even considering buying something?

In Chapter 1, you wrote down what you value. You thought about your life, your family, your future, and wrote down what's important to you. That was the first big step in combating impulse and overspending. By having a narrow focus on what you want and value, you are trimming your focus so just the important things meet your criteria. Think of the relationship between your brain and what you value as a funnel. In the funnel, there are a bunch of items and categories—travel, kids, education, new cars, designer goods, etc. As the items enter the funnel, your brain acts as a screen. It keeps the things you truly value moving down the funnel and stops the things you don't truly value from moving any further. Only the things that truly matter in your life make it all the way through the funnel. This is why it is so important to assess your values from the start. Your assessment of values will work for you to screen out the things you don't want and allow the things you do want to make it through.

Value Funnel

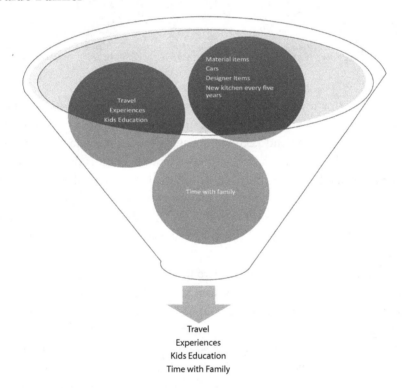

Travel
Experiences
Kids Education
Time with Family

To effectively use your value funnel requires that you train and coach your mind to stay focused on only the things you really want. Once the first step of assessing your values is complete, the rest is simply being mindful and consistent. For every purchase you consider making, your brain will give you an increase in dopamine. You'll get a momentary high, then the rubber really meets the road: You'll have to make a decision. Whenever the decision point hits, ask yourself the question, "Does buying this align with my goals and values?" If the answer is yes, you can make the purchase. If the answer is no, don't buy it. It's really as simple as this. Here's what to expect:

Spending Assessment Model

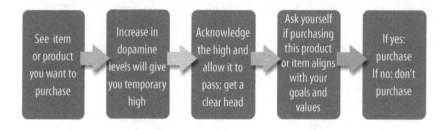

Following this model will almost act as a coach to align your spending with your values. Knowing what to expect *before* it happens will eliminate the surprise element and keep you focused. You'll already know why you want to make the purchase. You know that your brain is increasing your dopamine levels, giving you the urge to spend. You know that companies are spending billions of dollars in advertising to get you to purchase their products. Mentally going through this model and knowing what to expect will help keep you focused. This model allows your value funnel to work for you.

In summary, you are utilizing two tools here. The value funnel is something you create *before* having the urge to spend. It is your values and goals and what is really important to you. You established it with a clear head and gave yourself time to think about it. The spending assessment model is something you will use *in the moment.* It is the tool to use during the moment of truth when you are deciding whether to purchase something or not. It is your ally in impulse buys. If you go through the process, you are much more likely to make a decision that aligns with your values. Going through the short process allows you to acknowledge the temporary high, clear your head, then move on to your decision.

It's Not About Deprivation

Moving toward gaining control of your personal finances is not about deprivation. Sacrifices and choices, yes, but not deprivation. Nobody should feel deprived during their financial journey. If you feel deprived, that means your values are out of alignment with your spending choices or that your life perceptions are out of balance. They are two different issues that result in the same feeling of deprivation.

In situation one, you can afford something, choose not to buy it, and then feel deprived. In this case, your spending is out of line with your values. You were able to afford something but did not act according to your values. The result is the feeling of deprivation. In situation two, you cannot afford something, do not buy it, and then feel deprived. In this case, your values are out of balance with your life perceptions. Again, the result is the feeling of deprivation. These are two separate issues that end in a similar feeling. Situation one requires a change in behavior, and situation two requires a change in mindset, perception, and some may say reality. Take the following examples:

1. Not Acting According to Your Values

Scott is a big saver. His goal is to be financially independent within five years. He has eliminated unnecessary costs everywhere and has even taken on a few side hustles. He has tunnel vision toward attaining one goal—financial independence. Scott recently got an email from his old college buddies about going on a football trip, sort of a reunion with a sports theme. All the guys were going, even the ones with three or four kids. Scott really wanted to go, he had not seen the guys in years, and thought the trip would be a blast. It was going to be a great game too—the San Francisco 49ers vs. the New Orleans Saints in the New Orleans Superdome. Both teams were playoff-bound, and the winner of this game would be in the driver's seat for the number one playoff seed. After the game they would all head out for dinner and drinks in the French Quarter.

Despite really wanting to go to the game and easily being able to afford it, Scott emailed the group back with, "Sorry guys, would love to go but a little low on finances this year. Maybe next time. Have fun. –Scott"

Scott was disappointed and regretted his decision in the weeks leading up to the game. He truly felt deprived and wondered if this whole saving and investing money thing was worth it. Even a few months after the trip, Scott would sometimes reflect and kick himself for not going. The guys were still talking about it and Scott felt like he really missed out.

What went wrong with Scott in this scenario? He was easily able to afford the trip and really wanted to go. Yet he emailed back that he couldn't go this year. His spending habits were completely out of alignment with his values. Scott really valued spending time with his friends and wanted to go to the game, but he *did not follow his values.* The trip made it through his value funnel, but he did not act accordingly. He felt deprived and started to question his choice to pursue financial independence.

Decisions that are incongruent with your values will lead to feelings of deprivation like Scott experienced. These decisions are also more likely to derail future financial plans because they create an unsustainable lifestyle. That's why it is so critical to develop clear values and let them drive your financial decisions. A clear value system will put your financial decisions on autopilot, giving you a much greater chance to reach your goals.

2. Faulty Life Perceptions

Brian is a 24-year-old guy just a couple years out of college. Four months ago, Brian got a phone call from Stacy, his longtime girlfriend. Stacy wanted to break up. She had moved to New York City for a job after college with the idea that she could come back to Los Angeles after a year or two. She and Brian did the long-distance thing a little over a year but Stacy wasn't having it anymore. She told Brian she wanted to be single and just needed some time to experience the city unattached. Brian was devastated. After a few months, Brian decided he was ready to be over Stacy. Part one of his plan was to get a new luxury car to show the girls in LA just how well he was doing.

Brian went to the dealer, test drove the newest model, and sat down with the salesman. It would cost $47,500 out the door with the upgraded package. The salesman ran Brian's credit and asked him about a down payment. Brian told the salesman he could put down $3,500 on his credit card (he couldn't really afford $3,500 but thought it would make him a stronger buyer). The car lender came back and said they would only lend Brian $14,000. Brian was shocked and upset. He had a stable job and got by every month. He was baffled as to why the lender wouldn't give him the needed amount. Brian left the dealership, slowly got back into his car, and drove away. The whole way home, and for the next few days, Brian felt like he had been cheated out of a car he deserved.

Much like the deprivation Scott experienced, people can also experience deprivation by faulty life perceptions. Brian's feeling of deprivation is due to faulty life perceptions. He was looking to spend way above his means on a car that he was not even close to being able to afford. There was no evidence to suggest that he actually could afford this luxury vehicle. This type of situation can be mostly avoided by objectively and accurately looking at your circumstances. Take a step back and look at your situation from an outside perspective. Minimize or remove the emotion and base the situation on facts.

Value-Based Spenders

For the last three years, Cheryl has been looking to simplify her life. Her closet was full of clothes and shoes she barely wore. Weekends weren't much fun anymore, and she felt like Friday and Saturday nights were draining her bank account while providing little enjoyment. She also felt like she was spending a lot of money on lunches that all tasted the same; she thought to herself that a sandwich from home would probably taste just as good as one from a restaurant.

One Friday night in February, Cheryl decided to skip going out with her friends and instead looked through her finances. She was curious as to what was holding her back financially. She had a relatively high-paying job but was barely saving any money. Cheryl couldn't quite put her finger on it, but she thought the weekend nights out and lunches were probably the biggest drain on her bank account. She was shocked to find out that these two things were only a piece of her financial puzzle. Here are the highlights of what she found out by going through last month's expenses and writing them down:

- Going out on weekends: $375
- Lunches: $290
- Morning coffee and snack: $260
- Magazine subscriptions: $80
- Two gym memberships: $110
- Dinner take out: $280

- Clothes and shoes: $310
- Internet and TV: $130
- Cell phone and data: $120

Cheryl knew she was spending a lot on nights out with friends and frequently going out to restaurants for lunch. She was really surprised, shocked actually, to learn how much she spent on her morning coffee and snack, dinner take out, and especially clothes and shoes.

She began thinking to herself, "If I didn't even know I was spending this much on coffee, take out, and shoes, that means I didn't really enjoy these things." Cheryl concluded that if she was going to spend her hard-earned money, she should at least realize what she spent it on and enjoy it. That night, Cheryl decided to make some changes. From then on, other than necessities, she was only going to spend money on things she really enjoyed and valued. Cheryl stopped going out every weekend night. She still went out but only when she was excited to go out. Cheryl noticed those nights were really fun and she didn't miss the nights she didn't go out. She started cooking more and eating less take out. She stopped going shopping when she was bored. She went through her whole list and cut out every little thing that wasn't a necessity or was giving her joy.

A few months later, again on a Friday night, Cheryl went through her monthly expenditures to see what kind of progress she was making. She had spent almost $1,500 less that month than just a few months before. Half of it was going into an account to buy a home and the other half in a low-fee index fund. The funny thing is, Cheryl really didn't miss any of the stuff she used to spend her money on. In fact, it was the opposite. She enjoyed *not* spending because she felt like it simplified her life. Everything she spent money on now was intentional and thought out. She enjoyed her money by being intentional and frugal; she is now a value-based spender.

Value-based spenders know that gaining control of your personal finances should be fun and satisfying, almost the exact opposite of deprivation. The act of tracking money, planning, formulating ideas and strategies, watching strategies work, etc., should be highly satisfying in of itself. Financially successful people have learned that the process is inherently rewarding and that the result is only part of it. They are value-based spenders; their values are clearly defined and every decision is guided by those values.

By being intentional and deeply assessing her values, Cheryl became a value-based spender. She moved away from some of the things she used to spend money on for no reason. She cut out things she didn't enjoy anymore, like going out each and every weekend night. She discovered old gym memberships and subscriptions that she never used. Those things added no value to her life so she cut them out. Notice that Cheryl didn't just completely cut everything out and become a recluse. She found what she valued and kept those things.

Hedonic Adaptation

How many times have you walked into a friend's house or an open house around town and said, "I want this house!" You love the new kitchen countertops, the hardwood floors, and the oversized shower. You can picture backyard barbecues and your kids playing in the grass. Life would be unbelievably amazing if you had this house. However, the reality is that you already have most of what you love in your current house. You already have the big backyard and an area for the kids to play. Your kitchen countertops are a little dated but they look good. Your shower isn't oversized but there's more than enough space for you.

You think back to when you first bought or rented your current house. You felt the exact same way as you do now. You loved everything about it. You vowed you'd never move. This feeling usually lasts less than a year. This is called the hedonic adaptation. It basically says that whenever you get something new, you have a moment of time in which you are very happy about that particular purchase before returning to your original baseline of happiness. According to the social psychologist Heidi Grant Halvorson, the same phenomenon occurs with lottery winners and someone in a new job making more money.[2]

This phenomenon is normal. The problem occurs when you give in to expensive impulses to create a temporary feeling of happiness. If you act on it, those expensive impulses impact your life goals. For example, if your goal is to have financial freedom in the next 10 years but then you buy a brand new expensive home that is way out of your budget, you are derailing that goal for short-lived happiness. Fortunately, according to Grant Halvorson, there are two solutions for this phenomenon.

---

2   Heidi Grant Halvorson, "How to Keep Happiness From Fading," *Psychology Today* (August 15, 2012), https://www.psychologytoday.com/us/blog/the-science-success/201208/how-keep-happiness-fading

The first solution is to add variety and surprises; in other words, keep things fresh. For example, think back to the house I described earlier that you used to love but is now looking and feeling stale. Instead of buying a completely new house or remodeling the kitchen, try rearranging the kitchen or giving it a deep clean to bring out the original shine. Maybe declutter to open it up. Even cleaning the blinds or sink can add new life. These simple acts add new variety and life to your tired kitchen. Same thing with a car. Try taking your old car and adding some new life into it by deep cleaning the seats, vacuuming it, or using a new product on the tires and dash to get back the original shine. These acts will give you the positive emotions similar to purchasing something brand new.

The second suggestion from Grant Halvorson is appreciation. She suggests going out of your way to appreciate and be grateful for what you have. For example, when you walk into your house after a day at work, really notice and appreciate the space you have. Look at the open design of your kitchen and living room. Look into your backyard and appreciate all the open space and developed landscaping. Sit on your patio and enjoy the outdoor space. Think back to when you first bought or rented your living space and remember how much you liked it.

These two suggestions from Grant Halvorson directly align with an assessment of your values, a reoccurring theme in this book. A deep assessment of your values leads you to understand what is really important in your life. An appreciation of what is really important in your life helps you maintain happiness. For example, if you wrote down in your value assessment that you highly value time with family, take a moment each day to reflect how lucky and fortunate you are to be able to spend time with your family that day. In other words, being mindful and practicing gratitude for what makes you happy will help maintain and even increase your happiness. None of that costs any money, it is all about your mindset.

Frugality and Value-Based Spending in One Paragraph

Value-based spending is simply assessing what is important and then spending accordingly. It means weeding out the unimportant things and narrowing down what you really want. As you get better at assessing your values, it becomes almost easy to become a value-based spender. The tools in this chapter like the value funnel and the spending assessment model will help you become a value-based spender more quickly and efficiently.

Action Step

Name one spending habit that does not align with your values and take the steps to change the habit.

CHAPTER 3

Don't Compare Yourself to the Joneses, Because the Joneses Might Be Broke

Too many people spend money they haven't earned, to buy things they don't want, to impress people that they don't like.
– Will Rogers

Mark and Rachel Jones began dating five years after they graduated college. Fast forward another five years and you've got where they are today. They have a seemingly perfect life—two kids, a dog, good jobs, brand new cars, and a big house in a beautiful neighborhood. Both Mark and Rachel post photos and videos on Instagram at least three times a week of them going out to new restaurants, a new car by the lake, the kids playing in front of the house, and the high-end weekend getaways they take every few months. Their life seems like a revolving highlight reel. Many of their friends try to keep up with Mark and Rachel Jones. More than one of their friends have commented that they have a "perfect life."

However, outside of the walls of Instagram and Facebook is a much different story. Between posts, the Joneses constantly argue and bicker. Mark hates his job and Rachel works late most nights as a corporate attorney, frequently staying at the office later than 8:00 p.m. Most nights, Mark takes the kids out to fast food or orders takeout. After a long day, the last thing he wants to do is cook. Rachel sometimes eats at work or will have leftovers at home if Mark and the kids do takeout. When Rachel gets home, Mark usually snaps at her for leaving him with the kids again, and Rachel snaps back that she's been working all day and could really use a real meal now and then.

The long hours might be worth it if they were getting ahead financially, Rachel often thinks. The reality, though, is they have accumulated more than $23,500 in credit card debt, have two very large car payments, and a house payment that sometimes feels overwhelming. Childcare costs are also out of control, and it's going to be worse next year when their oldest starts private school. Rachel and Mark have both talked about being "one paycheck away from doom." Despite both Mark and Rachel having good salaries, they are living paycheck to paycheck and have seemingly insurmountable debt. They are both unhappy and have separately contemplated what life would be like if they were divorced.

Highlight Reel

Social media is a highlight reel. Instagram and Facebook posts show the best of the best. Posts are also written as the person posting wants them to be perceived. It is easy to spin posts, to make it seem like life is perfect. The fictional account of Mark and Rachel Jones is not far-fetched from the life of thousands of others. Reality is much different than a lot of people are letting on. The concept of "keeping up with the Joneses" has been around for years, but it's even more relevant today with social media.

One of the biggest problems with social media is that it leaves you comparing your everyday life to other people's highlights. It's like comparing apples to oranges, which is not a fair comparison. Of course, your ordinary day of getting up early, feeding the dog, taking the kids to school, and then going off to work will never hold a candle to the Joneses' posts of their Hawaiian vacation. It can get downright depressing comparing your everyday life to other people's highlight reels. It's unproductive and an unfair comparison. So don't do it.

Clinical psychologist Loren Soeiro writes in a 2019 article, "Survey studies have suggested that Facebook use leaves over 60 percent of users feeling inadequate."[3] He goes on further to write that any kind of compar-

---

3   Loren Soeiro, "Is Social Media Bad for You?" *Psychology Today*, (June 21, 2019), https://www.psychologytoday.com/us/blog/i-hear-you/201906/is-social-media-bad-you

ison against other people has a negative effect on your mood. This includes comparisons in which you judge yourself more favorably than others.

Comparing yourself to others is a trap to be avoided at all costs. The only comparisons you should be making is the progress you've made against your former self. Ralph Waldo Emerson writes, "To be yourself in a world that is constantly trying to make you something else is the greatest accomplishment." Oprah Winfrey writes, "You don't have to do what everyone else is doing." What the Joneses are doing has no bearing on your life. Whether they had a great vacation or not, will not make you any more or less successful. Comparing yourself to them is a waste of time and energy and gets you sidetracked from your goals.

The Crowd

When it comes to personal finances, don't be afraid to go against the crowd. The statistics on "the crowd" are not good. Millions of Americans are in debt and millions more have no savings. Look at these statistics from Debt. com and ask yourself if you should follow the crowd:[4]

- A 2018 study by Bankrate found only 39 percent of Americans have enough in savings to cover a $1,000 emergency.
- A report by SmartAsset finds the median net worth for Americans age 35–44 is $14,226.
- As of February 2017, the Federal Reserve listed the average personal savings rate in the US at 5.6 percent.
- A 2017 report in MarketWatch found that half of American households currently live paycheck to paycheck and that 49 percent of Americans are "concerned, anxious, or fearful about their current financial well-being."
- According to Y Charts Investment Company, Americans hold over one trillion dollars in credit card debt ($1,023,000,000,000).
- A 2017 CNBC article revealed that 157 million Americans have credit card debt to pay off.

Still want to follow the crowd? Following the crowd has never worked and definitely does not work when it comes to your personal finances. A huge issue rarely talked about in the personal finance space is that the "crowd" can

---

4   "Personal Finance Statistics: Compare Your Finances to Financial Statistics for the Average American Household to See How You Stack Up," *Debt.com*, (June 12, 2020), https://www.debt.com/statistics/.

paint a very different picture than reality. Take, for example, being great in a sport. It's hard to fake being great in a sport. The average person can tell very quickly if someone is a great basketball or softball player. A great basketball player can seemingly score at will, play great defense, and rebound the ball well. A great softball player plays excellent defense, can run, and can hit the ball hard most of the time. There really is no faking it. The average spectator can sit and watch a game and identify who is a great player.

Financial success, on the other hand, is actually pretty easy to fake. With the seemingly endless opportunities to borrow money, the average person can get themselves into a spiral of debt and buy things that make them look successful. Many people can finance a luxury car, an expensive wardrobe, jewelry, and other items, but the reality is that you don't know if these items have actually been paid for or if they are financed.

The person with these items, whether they are paid for or not, is giving off the perception that they have money to spend. In other words, it is easy to give others the impression that we have money to spend and are financially successful. Yet another reason to avoid keeping up with the Joneses. We don't even know what the comparison is because we don't have access to their financial information; all we see is the exterior picture of wealth they have painted for us. It is a waste of time to follow a crowd playing by all sorts of different and unknown rules.

Impressing Others

The concept of "keeping up with the Joneses" comes with an undercurrent of trying to impress others. Buying anything for the sole reason of trying to impress others is a bad idea. A really bad idea. Look at it this way: How many people do you think about daily for an extended period of time? Really think about it. Maybe your parents, kids, or spouse, but that's about it. I don't think many of us sit around at night thinking about how impressed we are with others. And I'll bet that there aren't a lot of people sitting around at night thinking about how impressed they are with you either.

This isn't to say you aren't an important person, it's just that nobody is so important that others are putting in significant amounts of time thinking about how impressed they are with you because of all the things you have purchased. Buying a bunch of stuff to try to win approval doesn't work. So the next time you think about buying something to impress someone else, don't do it.

Associate, but Don't Compare

We all know not to compare ourselves financially to the Joneses or the crowd. It's unhealthy and unproductive to compare finances. However, a great way to increase your likelihood of being financially successful is by associating with people who have achieved financial success. Notice the word selection: *Associate* with people who have achieved financial success. *Associate*, but don't compare.

Jim Rohn, a motivational speaker and business coach, said, "You are the average of the five people you spend the most time with."[5] Think of getting in shape, as in physical shape. If you hang around people who all exercise and eat well, you are much more likely to exercise and eat well yourself. If you meet a group of friends at a restaurant and all five of your friends order chicken or tofu, you probably will not be ordering lasagna, an appetizer, and a big dessert. If the majority of your friends hike, swim, and bike most weekends, you probably won't sit on the couch and binge watch Netflix on Saturday and Sunday. Birds of a feather flock together. The same principle applies to being in great financial shape. The more you associate with people who are in good or great financial shape, the more likely you are to be in good or great financial shape. It is a natural human tendency to assimilate with friends you spend the most time with.

Remember, you are not comparing your wealth to others. You are simply making efforts to associate with those who are skilled and disciplined in their personal finances. Iron sharpens iron. Lift up others around you and allow others to lift you up. Spend more time with successful people. Associate, but don't compare.

Maintain Your Power

Comparing yourself to others and trying to keep up with the Joneses takes away your power. Your true power in life lies in maximizing your own potential. Trying to chase and impress others takes away from that focus. Your power should instead come from setting personal goals according to your values and taking everyday action toward those goals. That is how you will accomplish things. The Joneses' goals are not the same as yours, so why would you chase them?

---

5   Aimee Groth, "You're the Average of the Five People You Spend the Most Time With," *Business Insider*, (July 24, 2012), https://www.businessinsider.com/jim-rohn-youre-the-average-of-the-five-people-you-spend-the-most-time-with-2012-7.

Focus is critical in the pursuit of your happiness and goals. Things like trying to keep up with others and worrying about problems you can't solve take away from your focus. The less focus you have, the less power you have. The next time you realize you're comparing yourself to others or trying to impress someone, think about the time you are wasting and the negative consequences you're creating in your life. Maintain your power by focusing on yourself and what you can control.

Compare Yourself to Yourself

One of the best ways for you to improve yourself is by comparing who you are today versus the person you were last month, a year ago, two years ago, etc. This direct comparison will help you monitor the progress you made. This is one of the highest forms of accountability because it is a direct comparison of just you. It forces you to take a long hard look in the mirror. The only person in that mirror is you. People who are personally accountable are much more successful than those who take their power away by blaming others. Keep trying to improve yourself, avoid the trivial comparisons with the Joneses, and the results will come in abundance.

Action Step

Identify one person you compare yourself to and stop comparing yourself to that person today.

CHAPTER 4

Getting Out of the Paycheck to Paycheck Trap: Automating Your Savings and Paying Yourself First

Do not save what is left after spending; instead spend what is left after saving.
– Warren Buffett

Now that you've thought about and written down your values and goals, it's time to begin implementing the plan. The first step is to find a way to get out of the paycheck to paycheck trap that so many of us live in. Get up at 5:45 a.m., take a quick shower, feed the dog or cat, wake up the kids, rush through breakfast, then hustle to drop the kids off at school. Hit the drive through to get your bagel and coffee, rush in to work, off to the vending machine during morning break, out to lunch for a quick bite, back to work, leave at 5:00 p.m. to pick up the kids at soccer practice, then start thinking about dinner. Practice runs late, so you get takeout, gobble it down, then it's on to homework, bedtime, and a little bit of TV. Next morning, rinse and repeat.

The workweek was stressful, so you reward yourself with a sit-down dinner at your favorite local restaurant. Appetizers, dinner, drinks—it's no problem that the bill is more than $150 because you worked hard this week. You deserve it, you say to yourself. The next morning, you and the family go out to a quick breakfast before the soccer game. Pizza parlor for lunch then back home. Nobody really feels like cooking on a Saturday so takeout it is. Sunday is more of the same, except Sunday night is replaced by a family dinner with the grandparents at the Italian restaurant down the road. The bill is a little less than Friday night but it's still close to $100. Again, you tell yourself that you work hard and deserve to go out to dinner now and then. After all, $94 including tax and tip really is pretty reasonable for a family of four.

Where Did the Money Go?

At the beginning of the month, when it's time to pay bills, you look back on the month prior and wonder where the money went. There were no big trips or even weekend getaways for that matter. You didn't have to take the car to the shop and nothing broke in the house. So where did it all go? You and your spouse go through the bills and it all seems normal. About $600 went toward student loans, $450 for the SUV, $575 for the four door, $3,200 for the mortgage, $140 for internet and cable, some money for gas, and the rest on food. The food seems kind of high ($785 at restaurants, $845 grocery store, $390 fast food, takeout, and coffee shops) so you disregard it and say you'll just cut back a little next month.

For your New Year's Resolution a couple months back, you and your spouse decided you wanted to save more, but you were only able to save $125 this month. Slightly disappointed, you and your spouse again say you'll do better saving next month.

New Month, Same Problems

While your intentions are good, the next month presents some different financial challenges. On the eighth, the garbage disposal breaks and it costs $225 to hire someone to replace it. On the 14th, the car needs an oil change and the mechanic discovers a couple small oil leaks. That costs $385 to fix.

You can already tell money is going to be tight this month, so the big Friday dinner is replaced by takeout, "saving" $55. Again, at the end of the month, disappointment reigns. This month it was break even, but at least you didn't have to dip into savings for the car and garbage disposal. Just like last month, you tell yourself that next month will be different.

As the months pass, you find you either break even or save next to nothing. It feels like you are running in financial quicksand. You and your spouse continually ask each other how you can possibly get out of the paycheck to paycheck trap. The months of frustration have started to add up and both you and your spouse are very unsatisfied with the way things are going financially. All the time and energy at work is doing absolutely nothing to improve your financial situation. The New Year's resolution of saving more money has not gone well.

Automate Your Savings

The absolute best way to get out of the paycheck to paycheck cycle is to automate your savings. Many of us are diligent about paying others, always paying bills on time, never missing a payment. We show great respect for others but don't take care of ourselves. Good habits translate; take your financial habit of paying others on time and *start paying yourself first*. The concept of paying yourself first is foreign to so many people. It goes against what we have been taught about money. So many of us have been taught that money is meant to pay bills with and buy more things. Then you take what is leftover and "save what you can." This is completely backwards. It is imperative to pay yourself first, to make yourself the priority.

Most people get paid twice a month. The paycheck temporarily fattens up the bank account then it all goes away, leaving us with almost nothing. We don't even know where it went. *The key is to start paying yourself when you have the money to pay yourself.* Before you even have the opportunity to spend money, start automating. Set aside money in separate accounts for an emergency fund, cars, children's education, investments, and whatever else you value. Remember, what you value will come from what you decided in chapter one. Automate your savings by taking at least 20 percent of your income right off the top, with at least 10 percent going to investments.

The First Few Months

The first few months will be challenging, but you will learn to live with your new savings rate. You will find that you don't miss the money at all and actually find it very comfortable living with your new income. You'll wonder what you used to spend it all on. At the end of each month, you will start to feel good about how much you saved. Before you know it, the months turn into years and you have quite a bit of savings in your accounts, something you never would have dreamed possible just a few short years ago. See the chart below for how this works.

For our purposes, let's assume you're able to save 20 percent on $5,000 a month total take home pay after taxes for a two-income household. According to US Census Bureau data released in September 2019, real median household income increased to $61,937 between 2017 and 2018.[6] Using that data, $5,000 per month is a realistic number to use as an example. The naysayers will say a 20 percent savings rate is unrealistic. Don't listen to them, they are not on the path to financial success that you are. Remember, you already assessed your values and wrote them down. That set of actions alone eliminated a lot of the old, unnecessary spending you used to partake in. The total savings rate is over $1,000 a month, assuming a conservative 2 percent interest rate.

Total Monthly Income After Taxes	Emergency Fund	College/Education Savings (for those with children)	Car	Investments
$5,000	$200	$150	$150	$500

Total After 1 Year	Total After 2 Years
$12,111.63	$24,466.71

Congratulations! You went from saving almost nothing to over $1,000 per month with interest. After just one year, you already have over $12,000 in your accounts, assuming a 2 percent interest rate. You are well on your way to gaining control over your finances. While you are not there yet, you have a proven plan that is working. After only one year, you aren't rich but you are out of the paycheck to paycheck cycle.

Saving Is Rewarding

An observation many readers will have after looking at this chart is that you won't be able to retain all these savings over the years due to the nature

6   Gloria Guzman, "New Data Show Income Increased in 14 States and 10 of the Largest Metros," *United States Census Bureau*, (September 26, 2019), https://www.census.gov/library/stories/2019/09/us-median-household-income-up-in-2018-from-2017.html

of what you are saving for. There will be times when you'll have to dig into the emergency fund. However, as you get better with saving, you also get better with learning what to spend money on and what not to. You'll also find that most items you once thought of as an "emergency" can actually be paid for out of pocket, leaving the emergency fund untouched and able to grow faster. The fact is that most "emergencies" are not emergencies at all.

Your out-of-date, 50-inch flat screen TV not having the newest technology is not an emergency. Keeping the money you save will become a personal challenge; the reward for saving will become so great that you will consistently challenge yourself not to touch the money you have in your reserves.

The same principle applies to cars. As you watch your savings grow, you will likely challenge yourself to purchase a more reasonably priced vehicle with your hard-earned savings or keep your current car longer.

Using the example above, saving $150 per month for a car will provide you with over $1,800 per year with a conservative 2 percent interest rate. That's over $9,000 in five years and over $18,000 in 10 years. You're not going to want to exceed your savings, so you will naturally bargain shop for the price you want to pay. Cars are such a huge piece of the money puzzle that they have their own chapter later in this book. You'll see in that chapter how being smart about cars will completely springboard your monthly savings and eliminate unnecessary debt.

Pay Increases: A Powerful Tool

One of the most powerful tools to getting out of the paycheck to paycheck trap is compounding your savings to include pay increases. Using the same chart as the example above, we are now going to add in pay increases to show the power that saving pay increases can give you over the years.

For this chart, we are going to assume a conservative pay raise of 2 percent per year using the same $5,000 pay base, which is slightly below inflation. We'll also use a modest interest rate of 2 percent. To show the power of year over year savings in one category, we're going to allocate the 2 percent raises to just the investment fund category. However, you can allocate the additional money the best way you see fit. In sum, you are now saving 20 percent of the original $5,000 plus 100 percent of the pay increases each year. This is quite possibly the best way to grow your monthly savings to well over 20 percent. Using this simple system, you will be *investing* over $900 per month of your income by year five!

Power of the Pay Increase

Monthly Income After Taxes	Emergency Fund	College/Education Savings (for those with children)	Cars	Investments	Total After Years End
Year 1: $5,000 (Original amount)	$200	$150	$150	$500	**$12,112**
Year 2: Adding 2 percent pay increase. Total pay $5,100	$200	$150	$150	**$600 ($100 more than year 1)**	**$25,943**
Year 3: Adding 2 percent pay increase. Total pay $5,202	$200	$150	$150	**$702 ($202 more than year 1)**	**$41,311**
Year 4: Adding 2 percent pay increase. Total pay $5,306	$200	$150	$150	**$806 ($306 more than year 1)**	**$58,272**
Year 5: Adding 2 percent pay increase. Total pay $5,412	$200	$150	$150	**$912 ($412 more than year 1)**	**$76,882**

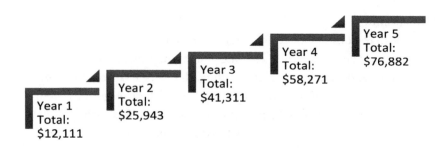

The power of combining pay increases with interest is clearly shown in this chart. After five short years, your financial situation has dramatically changed for the better. Your bank account has exploded from literally nothing to $76,882. That's not even factoring in that your investments, if invested properly, are going to earn you significantly more than 2 percent interest.

You are less than two years away from a six-figure bank account and light years away from the old paycheck to paycheck routine. No more frustration at the end of each month, you are fully executing your plan and see many years of growth ahead. Optimism reigns.

Allocating Money

As your accounts grow, you will also have great flexibility in determining how you want to allocate your money. Once you have a few months of an emergency fund saved up, you can reallocate those funds to something else. How much you want in your emergency fund is really on a case by case basis. For example, a tenured teacher with 20 years teaching experience can reasonably expect to maintain his or her employment without variations in pay. Conversely, a salesperson, whose income fluctuates monthly, would want to consider a larger emergency fund.

Once you hit your emergency fund number, you can reallocate the money. For example, if your child or children are approaching college age, you may want to put the money into the education fund. Or maybe you want to reallocate to the investment fund for a rental property or the purchase of more index funds. What and how to reallocate will be covered in Chapter 5. Now that you have financial flexibility, you have options. Options lead to increased opportunity and significantly less financial and overall stress.

With reallocation into different investment mediums, you will increase your average rate of return. Increasing your average rate of return will amplify your yearly returns. As of this writing, the average rate of return for an online savings account is a little under 2 percent. The average rate of return on a Vanguard Index Fund since its inception in 1976 is slightly over 11 percent.[7] To be conservative, we will use a 10 percent rate of return. To show the power of a higher rate of return, we will compare 2 percent to 10 percent side by side. Using an even number, we will start both accounts with $1,000 and contribute $200 monthly for 30 years.

	Year 1	Year 5
2% Online Savings Account	$3,468	$13,844
10% Vanguard Index Fund	$3,740	$17,728

Year 10	Year 15	Year 20	Year 30
$28,024	$43,680	$60,966	$101,122
$44,669	$88,057	$157,934	$451,714

As shown in this chart, the real compounding starts when you can get a higher rate of return. The rate of return matters a lot. The difference between earning 2 percent versus 10 percent is astounding. After one year it isn't much different, but as you get past five years, your money will grow exponentially faster in a higher producing investment vehicle.

By year 15, the 10 percent rate of return will have doubled the 2 percent rate. In year 30, you will have more than four times the amount. That's without any extra work, having to save any more money, or even having to think about it. The simple act of being intentional with your money, funding an emergency account, and then reallocating your money to a higher rate of return will produce incredible results.

Emergency Account, or Investments First?

The question so many people have is if they should completely fund an emergency account before beginning investing. Depending on who you ask, you will get different answers. Some will say you should completely

7   "500 Index Fund Investor Shares," *Vanguard*, (June 30, 2020), https://institutional.vanguard.com/web/cfv/product-details/fund/0040

fund your emergency account before even thinking about investing. Others will say to start investing now and use your investments as an emergency fund (and paying early withdrawal fees). My answer is to do both at the same time but allocate pay raises toward investments.

It's very important to have liquid cash on hand in case of an emergency. If the car radiator goes out, you want to be able to pull out a quick $500–$1,000 to pay for it without having to go into credit card debt or pay early withdrawal fees from your investments. For this reason, I like to have enough of an emergency fund on hand that I can access quickly. That way, emergencies are covered up to a certain dollar amount.

As we saw in the chart above, the power of compounding interest at a higher interest rate gives you massive returns versus lower rates closer to 2 percent. For this reason, it is important to invest while you are building up your emergency fund. The earlier you start investing, the more that time and compound interest works for you. With frugality and thoughtfulness, your emergency fund *will* get fully funded, it will just take a little longer because you're investing at the same time.

Progress Toward Success

Having executed a tried and true saving plan for several years, you are now working and investing with a purpose. Getting up early, fighting traffic, and dealing with stressors at work are giving you a significant financial reward at the end of each month. Your sacrifice has a meaningful financial purpose. By this point, you are far away from the paycheck to paycheck trap you were in only a few short years ago. Your mind is clear and it just seems easier to breathe these days. The stress and frustration you used to carry are replaced by optimism and accomplishment.

Action Steps

Open an online savings account and automatically have money withdrawn monthly. You can withdraw directly from your paycheck or from your checking account. Create sub-accounts for the things you value, for example: emergency fund, fun money, or vacations.

CHAPTER 5

Reallocating Money to Create Long-Term Wealth

The mind moves in the direction of our currently dominant thoughts.
– Earl Nightingale

Getting out of the paycheck to paycheck rut will provide you with tremendous financial flexibility. You will have a newfound freedom to use your money to meet short- and long-term goals. More importantly, you will be able to put more money into income producing assets, which will help you earn even more money.

The reallocation of funds comes in three primary forms—movement between accounts, debts paid off, and new income earned. Each is an equally important strategy and combining all three leads to exponential growth.

Movement Between Accounts, or Reallocating Money

After you have funded your emergency fund to your satisfaction, you can begin to move the money to other accounts. You can also create a hybrid reallocation where you still contribute to the emergency savings but contribute a different amount since it is already sufficiently funded. For example, if you have been contributing $300 per month to an emergency fund and met your goal of three months' savings, you can adjust your contribution to the emergency fund. Maybe you put $100 per month to the emergency savings with the remaining $200 allocated to your investment account, or put $50 per month to emergency savings and $250 to your investment account to name a few strategies. It is critical that you do *not* reallocate to daily living expenses—that's how you fall back into bad habits!

The chart below provides a few strategies on how you can reallocate from one fund to another. Using the example above, you have met your goal of three months of income in your emergency fund and are ready to move your contributions away from the emergency fund into another account.

	Former Contribution to Emergency Fund (Monthly)	Former Contribution to Investment Fund (Monthly)	New Contribution to Emergency Fund (Monthly)	New Contribution to Investment Fund (Monthly)	Total Contribution (Monthly)
Sample Strategy One	$300	$300	$100	$500	$600
Sample Strategy Two	$300	$300	$75	$525	$600
Sample Strategy Three	$300	$300	$50	$550	$600

Debts Paid Off

The second reallocation of funds will come from former debts you have paid off. Once you pay off all your targeted debts, you now have money to move into your savings and investment accounts. The key again is to immediately reallocate the money into the accounts you have created. If you don't, there's an excellent chance you'll get used to the new money and just spend it. Don't let yourself fall into this trap, make sure to immediately reallocate the money. Here's an example using different numbers than previous examples.

	Former Debt Payment on Student Loans (Monthly)	Former Contribution to Investment Fund (Monthly)	Former Contribution to Education Fund (Monthly)	New Contribution to Investment Fund (Monthly)	New Contribution to Education Fund (Monthly)	Total New Contributions (Monthly)
Sample Strategy One	$375	$100	$100	**$400**	**$175**	**$575**
Sample Strategy Two	$375	$100	$100	**$375**	**$200**	**$575**
Sample Strategy Three	$375	$100	$100	**$300**	**$275**	**$575**

Using this strategy, you have transformed a former debt payment of $375 per month into $575 ($375 + $200) per month saved and/or invested! You simply add the former debt payment to what you have already been saving and, voila, your monthly savings explode! This does not even include compound interest. To reiterate, the key is to immediately reallocate the money into a chosen fund to prevent the money from just going into your monthly living expenses and getting lost in the mix.

New Money

The third major reallocation of funds will come from new money. Pay raises, quarterly or yearly bonuses, tax refunds, gifted money, etc. As I wrote about in Chapter 2, pay raises will be allocated into investments. Infrequent increases in money such as bonuses and tax refunds will be allocated in one lump sum.

> *Evan gets a year-end bonus at work of $8,500, after taxes. He puts $7,200 into investments, $900 into the vacation fund, and $400 into the fun money account.*

In this example, Evan takes immediate and intentional action with the newfound money, $8,500 in this case. If Evan let the money sit in his checking account for a few months, at least half would be gone. Why? Because it's there and money without a purpose finds ways to get spent. Money just sitting in a checking account is like driving a car without knowing where you are going. If you don't have a place for your money to go, it will find somewhere to go on its own. By being intentional, Evan found a good home for his money where he'll be able to invest most of it and reward himself with a little extra vacation and fun money. Finding ways to increase your income or add new money is extremely powerful.

Finding New Money: Look for Ways to Increase Your Income

Think back to a time when you were planning on buying a car. More than likely you narrowed it down to a few different makes and models before coming to a final decision. What else happened during that time? I'll bet you started to notice the few cars you narrowed it down to much more often. "Hey, there's another Nissan Rogue," "I saw another Honda CRV at the intersection," or "that's the fifth Toyota RAV4 I saw in the parking lot at the store today." Why did you start noticing these cars? Were there coincidentally more on the road? Was there a sudden influx of people rushing to the dealership to purchase this class of vehicle?

What happened was that you trained and instructed your mind to look for the cars you narrowed your choices down to. You were on a mission and put your mind to the task of finding these cars on the road. This is the reticular activating system (RAS) at work.[8] The reticular activating system is not new. The original purpose was to help humans spot trouble—trouble like a hungry saber tooth tiger nearby that wants to eat you. The RAS was really a mechanism to avoid danger and death by tuning out the unimportant things and focusing on the things that really mattered, like a dangerous and hungry animal that wanted to eat you.

As humans have evolved, we use the RAS for more than just spotting dangerous animals. You can use the RAS to train your brain to look for what you really want it to look for. What if you instructed your brain to start looking for new and creative ways to increase your income, like new business opportunities or different ways to invest? Or maybe a new and more lucrative career path. Even cutting down your electric bill by installing solar at your home would qualify. What do you think your brain can find for you?

It's worth repeating the quote from the beginning of the chapter. Earl Nightingale wrote, "The mind moves in the direction of our currently dominant thoughts." If increasing your income is important to you, make it a dominant thought. Really think about how you can increase your income. It might mean a side hustle, new job, or entrepreneurship. Put some time into

---

8   Blaine Oelkers, "Unlocking The Screen of Your Mind: WYTAYBA," *TEDx*, (July 26, 2017), https://www.youtube.com/watch?v=xsrkOSTyWCU&t=329s.

thinking about it so that it becomes a dominant thought. Your mind will follow your directions and begin to work for you toward this goal.

Make increasing your income a state of mind, or a dominant thought. Allow your mind to work for you and find ways to increase your income. Don't confuse this with being singularly focused on money or greed. Remember to go back to your values to guide you in this mission. What do you value and how much money would help you obtain what you value? Then let your mind go to work and find it.

How Can You Increase Your Income?

When thinking about how to increase your income, start by asking yourself some questions: What are you good at? What do you like to do? What's a problem out there that needs to be solved? Put some time into working toward your answers, and you will notice the ideas start to flow. Ideas will come to you throughout the day—when you're walking, while you're driving, before you go to bed, when you wake up. Develop a system to capture these ideas.

A great system to capture your ideas and get organized can be found in David Allen's book, *Getting Things Done*. One of the central themes in the book is the idea of leveraging your "external brain," which is essentially a system to capture your important ideas and thoughts. Every time you have a great idea or thought, write it down. Allen's premise is that when you use a system to capture your great ideas, you won't bog down your mind trying to remember it all. In essence, you are giving your mind permission to keep coming up with great ideas because those ideas have a place to go. When your mind is free and clear to think and develop great ideas, it will work for you in new and exciting ways.

Peak Performance: Combining Strategies

You can increase your monthly income in multiple ways. Combining the strategies of reallocating your money, reducing your spending, and increasing your income will maximize your financial outlook. Combining all three methods, or even two out of the three, will create an exponential effect that will propel your personal finances to newer and greater heights.

For example, take someone making $4,000 per month after taxes. Suppose this person develops a side hustle that earns an extra $500 per month after taxes and business expenses. Now suppose this same person also found a way to reduce their spending by $750 per month. Their net difference with the side hustle and spending reduction is a highly impactful $1,250 per month! To make it even more powerful, if this person can reallocate money from another fund, they would increase their contributions even more.

If our example had only increased their income by $500, that would be the only gain. However, with the large spending reduction, the net gain is more than double and possibly could nearly triple with reallocated money.

This turbocharged boost to your personal finances began with a simple thought and a goal. Set a goal for your mind and it will find ways to help you reach your goal.

Be Realistic

When allocating money, make sure to be realistic. In the example with Evan, he put most of the money into his investment account but also put some aside for fun. It's important to find your balance between investing versus saving for fun things like vacations and the newest toy you have been wanting. Remember, allocating money is all about sustainability and consistency. Make sure you have the right balance between saving and living so you give yourself a chance to sustain the plan. In a way, your personal finances are like getting in shape. The person with the sustainable plan accumulates the money and keeps in shape. Those who use crash diets or stop spending any money cold turkey for two weeks usually fail. Create a sustainable plan for success—the tortoise wins the race.

Allocating money means you are being intentional with your money. Consistently allocating money year after year into investments is a formula for long-term financial growth and wealth. As your financial situation changes, it is your responsibility to closely track the changes and respond accordingly with the most appropriate reallocation. It doesn't take a lot of time or effort to do this but it's something that has to be done. Just a few minutes every month will be enough but it must be done consistently. This is part of the automation process. When you automate your money, you are being intentional by taking the time to set yourself up for success. The simple act of automating your money will set you up for financial success for years to come.

Action Steps

1. Develop one way to reallocate at least $100 into an investment. Take that action now.
2. Think of one way to increase your income.

CHAPTER 6

Automating Separate Accounts and Avoiding Lifestyle Creep

Put all of your savings on autopilot, and you likely won't notice the missing cash.
– Jean Chatzky

Being focused, looking for value, and maintaining an investment mindset can sometimes be taxing. We need tools to work for us on our journey. One of those tools is to automate our savings and investments. This automation will not only help you save money automatically but provide a holding place for different things you want to save and spend for. At a given point in the month, usually the first or 15th, automate payments to yourself in a few different areas. Investment money, travel money, fun money, an emergency fund, taxes, etc. Whatever you value or feel like you need to allocate for should have its own account.

Here's how it works: Suppose you make $4,000 per month after taxes. The first thing to do is pay yourself 10 percent first. That's $400 that goes straight into investments. Pay yourself even before you pay your bills. You must make a commitment to pay yourself first in the form of investing. Then assess your values and decide how you want to distribute the remaining money to yourself. Here's a sample of how to distribute the money. Remember, at least 10 percent needs to be invested. Not just saved but invested. In the example below, $400 is put into investments, equaling 10 percent, $275 is put into the emergency fund, $100 into college savings while the remaining money is put into fun things like the vacation and throwaway fund. All of the funds equal 25 percent, which in this case is $1,000.

Monthly Amount	Distribution Area
$400	Investments
$200	Vacation
$275	Emergency Fund
$100	College Savings
$100	Throwaway Fund (Fun Money)
$1,000	**Total**

The remaining 75 percent of your money can then be allocated for your living expenses like housing, cars, and food. With this method, you are learning to live on 75 percent of your income because you are paying yourself first. You don't even have an opportunity to spend your full paycheck. Separate accounts challenge you to really assess your values and force yourself to allocate money to yourself. People often find that they are not satisfied with just investing 10 percent when they break it down like this so they frequently will increase their investment rate. They learn to comfortably live on less than 75 percent of their income. This is a good thing. As you sit down and assess your values versus your spending, you will gain clarity.

Don't Forget to Live for the Day

Saving and investing can sometimes become a fixation. You set a goal and are going to reach that goal no matter what. You do everything it takes and then some. Before you know it, the days turn into years and you realize you forgot to enjoy the life you have. Set up controls and structure to avoid this mistake. A great way to do this is by intentionally allocating money towards a vacation fund and fun money and then using that money guilt free.

Every month, set aside a certain amount of money for vacations. Yes, that is correct, every month. A major principle in this book is establishing your values and then aligning your spending with those values. Setting aside money for vacations and trips follows this principle. Think about the kind of vacations you value. Do you like to take several mini vacations during the year, long weekend types of trips? Or do you prefer longer international trips? Or a combination of both? Understand your values then align your trips and experiences to those values.

After clear identification of your values, develop a vacation plan that aligns with those values. For example, if you value a long trip in the summer combined with several short trips during the year, like I do, think about where you'd like to go. Then think about the total cost and what that would break down to month by month. Do a double check to make sure these trips truly align with your values. Compare your travel and vacation values to your other financial and life goals. Find the balance that works for you, keeping in mind that your plan is expected to have travel and vacation expenses embedded into it.

When you have your number, set up an online account to automatically deduct money each month that will cover your costs. As the years go by, you will learn by trial and error how much you need every month. You will get into a rhythm and the saving will become easy and automatic. Setting up an online account that automatically deducts each month for vacations and trips will ensure that you get to take the trips you value. It also helps to eliminate some of those wasted vacations that you really never valued in the first place.

Rest, relaxation, and vacations helps rejuvenate your mind and body. Everyone needs to take a step back and relax. As counterintuitive as it might seem, taking vacations will help you move toward your financial goals. When your mind has an opportunity to relax and take a step back, it has a way of creating more and more ideas that will help you move forward on your journey.

Not only do vacations help you rejuvenate, but in their most basic form, they are fun. You have fun with your significant other, your kids, your friends, and your extended family. Life is supposed to have fun moments. Create as many fun moments as you can. If you plan ahead, fun moments do not have to break the bank.

Throwaway, or Fun Money

Moving toward your financial goals requires self-discipline and intentionality. It requires thought, aligning your values with your spending, and planning for success. Sometimes the process is difficult. There will be times you want to give up and go back to your old habits.

Give yourself a break and allocate a small amount of money each month to a throwaway account. Inevitably, there will be things here and there you'd like to buy that do not make a lot of sense. That's OK—that is what the throwaway money is for. Having throwaway money gives yourself permission have a slip up now or then. A night out with friends that ended up a little more expensive than you planned? That's OK, you've got it covered.

Finances are a major source of contention in marriages and long-term relationships. Throwaway money can drastically reduce marital discord. Think of it like this: You have your throwaway money and your significant other has theirs. You both can make any purchase (within reason) with the money guilt free. Throwaway money is especially great for personal hobbies that your significant other may not have an interest in. For example, if you love photography but your husband doesn't, you can use the fun money to buy all the photography equipment you want. An account like this also structures a set amount of money monthly that provides each person in the relationship financial autonomy. This system is easy to set up, does not require a major financial commitment, and there are many benefits.

Avoid Lifestyle Creep by Using Separate Accounts

Separate accounts will help you avoid the dreaded lifestyle creep. Lifestyle creep is when you unknowingly increase your expenses as you make more money. It happens slowly and without you even noticing. Every increase in pay goes to new expenses so you can't get ahead. Lifestyle creep is like the legend of the frog in boiling water. The story goes if you place a frog in a pot of water and turn up the heat slowly, the frog will stay in the pot of water, get used to the gradual increase in temperature, and eventually die. However, if you place a frog in a pot of water that is already boiling, the frog will be shocked at the heat and quickly jump out and save his own life.

Lifestyle creep follows the same concept. As your wages and earnings slowly increase, you will not notice your spending slowly increasing. Over time, though, such as a five- to 10-year period, there is an astonishing difference. Look at the following chart to see the true negative effects of lifestyle creep.

Lifestyle Creep

	Monthly Salary After Taxes	Monthly Spending	Net Monthly Savings/ Investments	Yearly Net Savings/ Investments
Year 1	$3,500	$3,300	$200	$2,400
Year 2	$3,605	$3,405	$200	$2,400
Year 3	$3,713	$3,513	$200	$2,400
Year 4	$3,824	$3,624	$200	$2,400
Year 5	$3,939	$3,739	$200	$2,400
Year 6	$4,057	$3,857	$200	$2,400
Year 7	$4,179	$3,979	$200	$2,400
Year 8	$4,304	$4,104	$200	$2,400
Year 9	$4,433	$4,233	$200	$2,400
Year 10	$4,566	$4,366	$200	$2,400

Assumes 3 percent yearly pay increase and the same monthly savings.

As the chart indicates, there is a massive difference between the year one monthly salary and the year 10 monthly salary. Of course, there will be a massive difference in net savings, right? Not with lifestyle creep. Even though the year 10 monthly salary is significantly higher than the year one monthly salary, the monthly spending increases in proportion to the pay increases. Thus, the monthly net savings remains stagnant, as does the total yearly savings. In other words, the person in this example is no better off financially in year 10 than they were in year one.

In actuality, the person in this example is worse off for two reasons, the first being inflation. The $200 he saved 10 years ago was worth more than the $200 he is saving today. Secondly, his expenses have gone way up, so he is now dependent on a much higher income than before. If there is a job loss or reduction in pay, this person will struggle to make ends meet. He or she has created a new lifestyle and has to make more money to just to keep up with that lifestyle.

Imagine if we showed the individual in this example the true power of lifestyle creep over a 10-year period. They would see an increase of over $1,000 in monthly income but no difference in savings. Seeing a statistic like that would probably shock and upset the average person. When it happens gradually, though, people barely notice the incremental changes. Suppose our friend in this example saved and invested proportionally to their pay increases instead of spending it. Let's take a look at what that would look like.

Lifestyle Creep Reversed

	Monthly Salary After Taxes	Monthly Spending	Net Monthly Savings/ Investments	Yearly Net Savings/ Investments
Year 1	$3,500	$3,300	$200	$2,400
Year 2	$3,605	$3,300	$305	$3,660
Year 3	$3,713	$3,300	$413	$4,956
Year 4	$3,824	$3,300	$524	$6,288
Year 5	$3,939	$3,300	$639	$7,668
Year 6	$4,057	$3,300	$757	$9,084
Year 7	$4,179	$3,300	$879	$1,758
Year 8	$4,304	$3,300	$1,004	$12,048
Year 9	$4,433	$3,300	$1,133	$13,596
Year 10	$4,566	$3,300	$1,266	$15,192

*Assumes 3 percent yearly pay increase.

The results are astounding. Just by saving pay increases, the person in this example has gone from saving $2,400 per year to $15,192 per year. That does not even factor in other methods of saving or compound interest. This is tremendously powerful and creates yearly sustainable investable cash flow.

The naysayers will argue that saving pay increases every year is not possible due to inflation and other increased costs of living, such as food, housing costs, gas, professional services, etc. However, if you can reduce your expenses by doing things like eliminating car payments and making housing a fixed cost, you have a much better chance to save all or most of your pay increases. For example, if you purchase your own home, your monthly principal and interest payment will not go up as long as you have a fixed rate. This is in contrast to renting, where you will have many rent increases over a long period of time.

It doesn't have to be all or nothing. Even if you save 80–90 percent of pay increases to account for inflation and increased expenses, that is still exponentially better than doing nothing. Or maybe you save 100 percent of four pay increases in a row and then put half of your fifth pay increase toward living expenses. Be creative, there are many ways to make saving and investing work for you. It is never all or nothing.

By investing as much as you can from your pay increases, you will eventually get to higher investment percentage rates. The important thing is to develop a plan and start taking action. And remember, there will always be doubters and people telling you why you can't do certain things. Take a careful look at some of these people: Are they financially successful? Are they really qualified to be giving you advice? How much of their pay increases are they saving and investing? Tune these people out and instead focus your efforts on interacting with people who are successful and actually encourage you to improve your financial picture.

Action Steps

1. Automate your savings. Set up accounts at the start of each month so that your money is automatically transferred to an investment account.

2. As soon as you get your next pay increase, have that money automatically transferred monthly to an investment account.

CHAPTER 7

Bad Debt, and How to Get Out of It

10% of the borrowers in the world use debt to get richer—90% use debt to get poorer.
– Robert Kiyosaki

Bad debt is sacrificing your future day needs for your present day desires.
– Suze Orman

Debt is arguably the most written about financial topic. It is also one of the most controversial and polarizing financial topics out there. Is all debt bad? What is good debt? Should you pay off your house or not? Is it ever OK to have a credit card balance? Should you do a cash out refinance to buy rental property, invest in the stock market, or some other type of investment? You will find there are many answers to the myriad debt questions. The key is to apply sound financial principles to the debt puzzle and do what is most beneficial for you and your family. The next two chapters will focus on debt and help you identify good debt, bad debt, and what to do about it.

Bad debt is arguably one of the most stressful things in the lives of Americans today. Debt can and will take a major toll on your health and relationships. When partners are out of sync regarding debt, relationships are often compromised. Debt can also weigh on us individually, adding unwanted stress to our daily lives. Debt can seem like a never-ending black hole, impossible to get out of. Bad debt keeps people in jobs they don't like and keeps people up at night. It is also one of the leading causes of arguments between spouses. Bad debt is consuming and stressful. So what can we do about debt? Start taking action against it!

In this chapter, we will assume there is bad debt to be paid off. The strategies outlined in this chapter are all geared to bad debt pay down and elimination. If you have bad debt, keep reading. If you have absolutely zero bad debt, congratulations, this is one chapter you may want to skip.

Identify Debt

Begin by writing down all your debts, interest rates, total debt, and monthly costs. This can be handwritten, put into a spreadsheet, or whatever method is most effective for you. Use the template below or create your own. The key is to do it. Writing down your debts will provide you with the first blueprint for the roadmap on how to attack and kill debt. Notice the second to last category is emergency fund contribution of $100 per month, followed by $50 per month in investments. While you are in the debt pay down phase, save at least $100 per month so you have an emergency fund to fall back on. This will act as a safeguard from going back into debt each time an unexpected cost comes up, which will happen. It may sound counterintuitive to build up your emergency fund, but without it, the debt will just continue to accumulate every time there is a financial need. Without fail, Murphy's Law seems to find those that have no emergency account to fall back on.

In addition, start investing now, even if you have bad debt that needs to be paid off quickly. There are two major reasons for this: The first is to get into the habit of investing. Habits form over time; they are not easy to turn on and off. Those who create the habit of investing early will continue that habit as they acquire more money and pay off debt. The second reason is to start allowing compound interest to work for you. Get the process started early so that you have the power of time on your side.

Here's a quick example of the power of time as it relates to compound interest. If Jennifer invests $1,000 when she's 20, that will have compounded to $45,259 by the time she is 60 years old, assuming a 10 percent rate of return. However, if Jennifer decides to wait and invest that same $1,000 at a 10 percent rate of return at the age of 40, she will only have $6,728 by the time she is 60. Time is incredibly powerful and should be taken advantage of as soon as possible so that money can compound. Get time on your side now—don't wait to invest, even if it's only a little bit of money at first.

Use the template below or create your own to write down all debts. Include the interest rate, balance, and minimum monthly payments.

Debt Type	Interest Rate	Balance	Minimum Monthly Payments
Emergency Fund	2% positive interest	N/A	$100
Investments	10% positive interest (average return)	N/A	$50
Total			

Example Template

Debt Type	Interest Rate	Balance	Minimum Monthly Payments
Credit Card 1	13.99%	$6,500	$260
Credit Card 2	11.54%	$7,800	$312
Department Store Card	11.55%	$495	$19.80
Jewelry Store Credit	6%	$800	$32
Furniture Store Credit	11.95%	$1,700	$68
Tire Store Credit	3.70%	$385	$15.40
Car Payment 1	2.80%	$27,455	$490.89
Car Payment 2	3.88%	$8,700	$159.75
Monthly mortgage	3.65%	$300,000 (not original amount of loan)	$1455.71
Property Tax and Insurance	N/A	Monthly	$350
Emergency Fund	2% positive interest	N/A	$100
Investments	10% positive interest	N/A	$50
Total	N/A	$353,835 (not including interest)	$3,313.75

Decide What Debt to Pay Off

Now that you have all your debts written down, now is the time to move on to action step number two, which is to decide what debt to pay off, what debt is acceptable to keep, and what debt you can rid yourself of quickly. For example, you can sell an expensive car and get one that's more cost effective to reduce what you owe.

In general, consumer debt is considered "bad debt" and should be put in the bucket of debt to pay off first. Consumer debt includes all credit card debt, including the big credit card companies, department stores, furniture stores, etc. Car payments are also bad debt and need to be put in the bucket of debt to pay first. The items in bold in the chart above are bad debt that needs to be paid off as quickly as possible.

Selling Things

Now that you have assessed your debt, the next action step is to literally start selling things that don't align with your values. Using the chart from above, you'll see that two huge sources of debt are the car payments of $27,455 and $8,700. Both debts would require many years of expensive payments. This is where your value assessment will be challenged. Do you really need the cars? Would a much less-expensive car serve your needs? Do you really need both cars, or can you sell one and keep the other? If you live in a big city with parking meters and parking garages, what is the car really costing you? Hint: it's costing you way more than just the payments and gas!

Let's look at the car with a balance of $27,455. After your down payment of $6,200, you are left with a monthly payment of $490.89 for the next five years. That money is all going toward a *depreciating liability* for a full five years. That's money that can't be put toward other debts, college savings, investments, or a savings cushion for five full years. Is it worth it? You may decide that it is worth it—maybe you love the car and it brings daily joy to your life during your commutes and road trips despite the financial consequences. Or maybe you decide it's not even close to worth it and all you really need the car for is short daily trips to work and picking up the kids. A much less expensive car would do just fine, assuming the car is reliable.

Continuing to use our $27,455 car balance as the subject, suppose you decide to sell the car so you can purchase a much less expensive one. You originally put $6,200 down and still owe $27,455. If you sold the car to-day, you could get about $29,000. Assuming you continue with your plan to sell the car, you'd be left with $1,545 after the sale of the vehicle. While that's not going to be enough to purchase a reliable car, it's a start. Victory number one is that you eliminated monthly car payments of $490.89 for the next five years. Victory number two is that you will be reducing your vehicle registration fees by a few hundred dollars per year. Victory number three is you will likely be reducing your monthly insurance premium. And if your next purchase is a car that gets better gas mileage, that is another victory.

Even though you just rid yourself of a $490.89 monthly car payment for five years, you now have a new problem. You need a car! Riding your bike or taking public transportation to work isn't a viable option in your case so you determine that you definitely need a car. The good news is that you have $1,545 from the sale of your last car, assuming you have no other money to contribute. So now it's time to purchase the replacement vehicle. The goal here is a reliable car with good gas mileage. Suppose you found a reliable car already checked out by a mechanic that gets above-average gas mileage for $9,500. Putting $1,545 down leaves you with a balance of $7,955 and a new monthly car payment of $142.24. That is a total debt reduction of $19,500 and monthly car payment reduction of $348.65! The beauty of this strategy is that you didn't have to pay down any debt or sac-rifice anything other than selling a car. Selling the car gave you a quick and extremely impactful victory. Eliminating years and years of expensive car payments is a huge victory than will propel your personal finances to new levels. Eliminating almost $20,000 of debt in one fell swoop is a huge deal!

You now have a good choice to make. You can either apply the addi-tional $348.65 to your replacement car or to another debt. Either way is a win, just make sure to immediately apply the money to another debt and not let it sit in your checking account where it will inevitably get spent on something else. As is almost always the case, any money "left over" in a checking account that doesn't have a plan will inevitably get spent on something else, completely defeating the purpose of the debt pay down. To make an apples to apples comparison, if you applied the additional $348.65 to your replacement car payment, your car would be paid off in less than a year and a half. That's three and a half years of payments saved!

65

Expensive Car vs. Inexpensive Car

	Monthly Payments	Number of Years
Keeping "Expensive" Car	$490.89	5
Selling "Expensive" Car	$490.89 (using money for replacement car)	1.5

Refinance and Negotiate Interest Rates

After you have sold what you can to eliminate debt, go through all your debt (both good and bad debt) and determine what you can refinance or negotiate into a lower amount. This is especially applicable to large purchases like real estate, cars, and credit cards with a high balance. Just reducing your interest rate by a small amount can give you big savings. As a quick example, look at the differences in monthly payments and total amount paid, for a house being refinanced with a $450,000 balance on a 30-year mortgage. As you'll see from the chart, it is clearly worth it to refinance to a lower rate if you can. Just a 1 percent change in the interest rate is worth hundreds monthly and tens of thousands over 30 years.

Payments for Different Mortgage Rates

$450,000 Balance	Monthly Payments	Total Paid Over 30 Years
3.5%	$2,021	$727,452
4.5%	$2,280	$820,830
5.5%	$2,555	$919,818

For credit cards, renegotiated rates can also provide significant financial benefits. For example, look at the massive difference interest rates make for a credit card with a $6,500 balance. A renegotiated rate from 18 percent down to 12 percent eliminates almost two years of payments and several thousand dollars.

Payments for Different Credit Card Rates

$6,500 Balance	Total Amount Paid	Years of Payments
12%	$8,600	10 years, 2 months
14%	$9,093	10 years, 8 months
16%	$9,647	11 years, 4 months
18%	$10,273	12 years

Debt Payoff Systems and Strategies

The next action to take is to begin paying off debt. Paying off debt requires using a system, of which there are several to choose from. We'll touch on a few common ways to attack debt, but there are many more out there.

The first is the "debt snowball" method popularized by Dave Ramsey. The second is the "debt avalanche," recommended by many financial authorities. Another way is via a hybrid system, taking principles from both strategies and applying them to a strategy that meets your needs. Any hybrid system will be highly individualized and look different for each person.

All systems work, and the most important thing to do is to pick one and take action. When people begin to get too fixated on what system to use and don't take action, it leads to analysis paralysis. Don't get too fixated on the system, just pick one and take action. Remember that the bad debt will get paid down but it does take getting started.

1. The Debt Snowball

The debt snowball combines debt payoff with basic human psychology. The idea is to pay off the smallest debt first to give yourself small wins and build confidence. With small wins and confidence, the theory is that you are more likely to keep paying off debts until you have no more debt. Using the chart above, we have exactly $3,313.75 of debt to pay every month (including contributing to the emergency fund and investments).

We'll continue to assume that monthly household earnings equal $5,000 after tax. After accounting for the money allotted for food, kids' activities, daily living expenses, etc., let's assume you have $3,429 left over to pay off $3,313.75 worth of debt per month. Using the debt snowball approach, you would pay the minimum payment on every item but the tire store credit, since that's your smallest debt, even though it has a low interest rate. Since you have $115.25 left over after monthly expenses, you would put in all $115.25 plus the minimum of $15.40, totaling $130.65 for the month. You would do this until the debt is completely paid off.

In approximately three months, the debt owed to the tire store credit card will be completely paid off. Victory number one! The next step is to take the $130.65 you previously put toward the tire store to the next smallest debt. In this case, it would be the department store credit card of $495. Now take $130.65 plus the minimum payment of $19.80 to equal $150.45. In a little over three months, the department store credit card would be paid off. Victory number two, and on to the next debt!

With the department store credit card paid off, you can now move on to pay off the jewelry store credit card. Take the $150.45 you were paying toward the department store and add it to the minimum payment of $32 on the jewelry store card, equaling $182.45. In a few short months, the jewelry store credit card will be paid off and you move on to the next smallest debt. Keep repeating this cycle until all debts are paid off. Psychologically, this is a superior strategy. The wins come early and often, and they are very easy to see. Your confidence builds, and it feels good to get the easy wins. Especially for people who have had little financial success, it feels great to start "winning" the personal finance game.

2. The Debt Avalanche

The second common strategy to paying off debt is called the debt avalanche, or debt stacking. In this strategy, pay off the highest interest rate debt first. It doesn't matter how much you owe, the only number you're looking at is the interest rate. This strategy will save you the most money if done correctly and consistently. The biggest drawback to this strategy is that the rewards can come very slowly if the highest interest rates also have the highest balances.

Those electing to use this method need to be very patient and consistent. Using this strategy can feel like you're not making progress, which can oftentimes lead to falling back to old debt habits, quickly derailing any progress toward debt reduction.

Let's take a look at an example of how the debt avalanche works. Using the same chart we used for our debt snowball strategy, let's now apply the debt avalanche strategy. The highest interest rate is credit card number one at 13.99 percent, with a balance of $6,500. Making the minimum payment of $260 plus the $115.25 we have left over each month for a total of $375.25, it would take a little over seven years to pay off this card. After this is paid off, you move on to the next highest interest rate debt and apply the same process until all debt is paid off.

Again, the main challenge to this strategy is the length of time it takes, which equals less frequent positive reinforcement toward paying off the debt. In the end you will have paid less than using the debt snowball, but many people are not able to stick to this method for years on end.

It is harder to gauge progress using this strategy, and it is not as rewarding as the debt snowball where you can clearly see the smallest debts being paid off quickly. While this strategy technically is the optimal way to pay off debt, it does not provide the frequent positive reinforcement that many people need in their debt payoff. Especially for those who are just learning about personal finances, this strategy can feel like walking in quicksand.

3. The Hybrid System

The hybrid system takes elements from both strategies and combines them into one strategy that works for you. For example, those using a hybrid system might start with paying off the smallest debts first, no matter the interest rate. Or in other words, the snowball method. This will help to build confidence and show tangible progress.

Once you build up sufficient confidence and see your progress, switch over to the debt avalanche strategy to optimize the debt payoff until it's completely paid off. The switch over will save you money in the long run. By combining systems, or using a hybrid method, you get the best of both systems. Confidence in the beginning to keep paying off debt and optimization later in the payoff.

Beware of the "Experts"

Many financial pundits, gurus, and "experts" will tell you it's their way or the highway to pay off debt. The truth is that most systems will work; the most important thing is to pick a system and get started. Whether it's the debt snowball, debt avalanche, or a hybrid method, pick one and move forward. You know your personality best and will be the best judge about what strategy is best for you and your family.

Debt Payoff Order for Each System

Bad Debt Type	Interest Rate	Balance	Order to Be Paid Off Using Debt Snowball	Order to Be Paid Off Using Debt Avalanche	Order to Be Paid Off Using a Hybrid System
Credit Card 1	12.99%	$6,500	5	2	6
Credit Card 2	13.54%	$7,800	6	1	5
Department Store Card	11.55%	$495	2	4	2
Jewelry Store Credit	6%	$800	3	5	3
Furniture Store Credit	11.95%	$1,700	4	3	4
Tire Store Credit	3.70%	$385	1	6	1
Car Payment 1	3.65%	$27,455 (if not selling)	8	7	7
Car Payment 2	2.80%	$8,700	7	8	8

Staying Out of Bad Debt

Bad debt is suffocating for millions of people. It's something that can sneak up over time, gathering negative momentum until it seems hopeless. This chapter gives you tools to get out of debt, but I recommend further educating yourself on this topic if you have significant debt. See Appendix A for further reading—there are many great books listed there. Additionally, Appendix B lists many great podcasts, and Appendix C lists some great websites and blogs on this very topic.

Once you're out of "bad debt," it goes without saying that you never want to get back into that kind of situation. The rest of this book will be focused on maintaining a healthy financial situation, which is naturally free of consumer debt, or "bad debt."

The New Graduate

Brian graduated from college in 2005 with a degree in communication. He went to work in a sales position making $40,000 plus bonuses right out of college. Most of his friends from college moved to different cities so Brian had to make new friends. This wasn't a problem for Brian, as he was very social and was sometimes described as the "life of the party." He often would be seen out late night at bars buying a round or two of shots for his buddies and even strangers. It wasn't uncommon for weekend bar tabs to exceed $200.

Most of Brian's friends at the sales firm were making good money and were driving expensive luxury cars. Brian felt like his car from college was inadequate, so he traded it in to purchase a new luxury car for $35,000. Before purchasing the vehicle, Brian worked out the numbers and figured out the maximum he could afford was $37,000, so he was happy to be "under" budget. The monthly car payments were $628.90 for five years, which he was able to "afford." That took away his monthly savings but he had a really cool car.

For the first year after college, Brian was able to pay off his credit card monthly. It was challenging but he always found a way. Brian thought he was doing fine because he was able to make his car and credit card payments. However, later that summer, his car needed $1,700 worth of re-pairs, which Brian literally did not have. He decided that he would put the repairs on the credit card and pay it off after his year-end bonus in Decem-ber. The next few months, the credit card balance ballooned to $3,200, as there were a couple more unexpected expenses. Still not a problem, Brian thought—the year-end bonus would wipe out all this unexpected debt.

As expected, Brian received his end of year bonus—$4,500 was a little more than he thought he would be getting, so he decided to book a va-cation to Hawaii with a girl he had met at a happy hour. Brian knew he still had the credit card to pay off, but he rationalized that he got a bonus and the Hawaii trip was a smoking deal. So Brian put $2,200 of the bonus toward the Hawaii trip and put the remaining $2,300 towards the credit card balance, leaving a more manageable $900 balance. Brian said to himself that he would take it easy that winter after the Hawaii trip so he could pay off the balance.

Throughout the fall and early winter, Brian found himself going out more with the girl he met at the happy hour. They were now officially dating. They were going out to nice dinners at least three times a week, and he was still going out with his buddies on the weekends. "Taking it easy" didn't happen that winter, and the credit card balance crept back up to $3,000+ before summer even began. Over the course of the year, the credit card moved all the way up to $7,500. Brian found himself struggling just to make the minimum payment on the card. He was starting to worry because even with his bonus, he still wouldn't be close to paying off his credit card.

Over the next three years, Brian maxed out his first credit card at $12,000, so he opened a second one. During that time, Brian had also sold his car to buy a slightly more expensive one, so he had another five years of payments at $670 per month. He still had no emergency savings and only had $750 in the bank. He was living paycheck to paycheck, struggling just to pay his bills. Things were getting more than uncomfortable, and Brian was feeling hopeless about his financial situation, despite getting a few raises. He didn't understand why he was so much worse off now than he was right after college.

Although fictitious, Brian's situation isn't unusual. There are many people who get out of college, trade schools, or get a recent promotion who have never made "good" money before. They are not used to this type of salary, so they begin spending, not realizing the massive hole they are digging. Before they realize what is happening, they are already in seemingly insurmountable debt. This can happen in as little time as a few months or over the course of several years. No matter how long it takes, "bad debt" is never a good thing. It is important to develop strategies to avoid this kind of debt, especially during transition times to higher paying jobs. An easy to implement strategy is to maintain your current standard of living at least six to 12 months after getting a big pay raise or a higher paying job. This will prevent that "feeling rich" syndrome that plagues so many people as they spiral into debt, even with higher paying jobs than they ever had before.

This "feeling rich" syndrome is a close relative of lifestyle creep, which will be addressed in later chapters.

Much like millions of other people, Brian got himself into a dire situation. If he does not act quickly, his debt will spiral completely out of control. Brian needs to put a quick end to his negative monthly cash flow. If you are in a position like this, make a plan to get out of it. If you are not in this type of position, pat yourself on the back and keep up the good work.

Action Steps

1. Fill out the debt chart.
2. Write down the debts you can simply sell off to eliminate. Sell those items within one month, starting with the most expensive items. This simple step alone may eliminate a great portion of your debt.
3. Refinance and/or renegotiate interest rates.
4. Pick a debt payoff strategy and stick with it until all bad debt is paid off.

CHAPTER 8

Credit Cards: To Use or Not to Use

Rich people use debt to leverage investments and grow cash flows. Poor people use debt to buy things that make rich people richer.
– Grant Cardone

Should you use a credit card? It's a simple question but with not-so-simple answers. There are so many mixed messages about credit cards. Credit card companies say that you should absolutely use them. You can pay off previous debts, have low introductory rates, and even get cash back and free flights. You would think from hearing their advertisements that you never even have to pay off their card! Others shout from the rooftops as loud as they can that credit cards are evil and should never be used. Cut them up! Burn them! So what's the truth?

The truth is that it depends. It depends on how responsible you are with credit cards. Are you the type of person who pays off their monthly bill without fail? Or are you the type of person who thinks you are getting free money because it's getting charged to plastic? Or are you somewhere in the middle; most of the time you pay it off but sometimes you have a late fee or get charged a few dollars in interest? Let's explore the benefits and drawbacks to using credit cards.

Benefits to a Credit Card

The reason I don't make a blanket rule about not using credit cards is that there are benefits to having one. Many cards offer airline miles, hotel rewards, cash back on purchases, and various other rewards. If you are responsible with your card, you can actually make money by using it. To clarify, this is not a pass to use your card for frivolous purchases and justify it by saying you get airline miles or cash back. What I mean by the statement is that you can make money from using credit cards on things you would be purchasing anyway such as food from the grocery store and clothes for your child. If you are going to buy it anyway, you might as well get some benefit is an argument that makes a lot of sense.

Rewards

Credit card rewards can be substantial. Many cards offer introductory deals in which a large amount of airline miles or points can be earned. Airline miles are valuable as they can basically be turned into cash when buying an airline ticket. Points can also be used for hotels, rental cars, flights, and myriad other items of value. Again, as long as the card is being paid off monthly, these perks are great and can benefit you as a consumer. If you love to travel, earning airline miles and free hotel stays are a great benefit. For each free flight or hotel, that's less money that you need to save for travel. Just don't allow yourself to get caught in the rationalization trap. Having the mentality of "I got this trip for free so I can go on an extra trip now" negates the benefit of the free trip. Even with airline miles and other credit card rewards, keep being intentional about travel.

Some consumers have even found ways to "buck the system" by systematically opening and closing multiple credit cards at strategic times. This is known as travel hacking and can be an effective strategy to earn more rewards. Travel hacking really does work but it requires skill, discipline, and organizational skills. If you are going to travel hack, make sure you have done the proper research and are confident in your abilities. There are many blogs and podcasts related to this topic. If you don't carefully track all your open cards, you can end up in a sea of confusion and unexpected debt.

Credit cards can also be especially useful if you own a business and make frequent purchases. The rewards add up if you use the right card for your business purchases. For example, a restaurant owner can use his card for food and alcohol purchases, furniture, decorations, and other items. As long as the balance is paid off every month, the restaurant owner can receive great benefit from the card. Or a real estate developer who purchases all of her materials with a credit card. If she uses her card to purchase the lumber, cement, fixtures, and countless other items, she can accumulate a lot of rewards. She can then use her reward miles to fly to other possible development locations, or even take the family on vacation, without spending a cent of her own money on travel.

Benefit or Myth?

The credit card companies advertise numerous benefits to using their card in addition to accumulating rewards. Are these really benefits exclusive to credit card holders or can the same benefits be found using other products or simply by returning the product? I argue that the majority of benefits can easily be found from other products or returning the item.

Purchase Protection

Many cards offer purchase protection. The reality is that many of the products already have purchase protections in place. Say for example that you purchase a lawnmower at the hardware store. A month and a half later the lawnmower breaks and will cost a few hundred dollars to fix. If you purchased with a credit card, many cards will reimburse you the money. And if you take the lawnmower back to the hardware store, they are also extremely likely to exchange it or give you your money back without much of an argument. Reputable stores will probably give you the same benefit as any credit card protection can give you in this type of scenario.

Tracking and Accounting

For tracking, you can use Mint or another money tracking app, or just track it manually yourself. You can hook up these apps to your debit card or manually enter the information—you don't have to use a credit card. It is convenient to use a credit card, but it's also just as convenient to use a debit card. You don't have to use a credit card to digitally track your money, plenty of other products offer it. To be honest, you can probably do the same thing with pen, paper, and less than 10 minutes a week. I'd argue that credit cards are the most convenient in this area, but for people who have challenges with paying their balance each month, this is not a great enough benefit to justify using a credit card.

Convenience

Credit card companies promote their product as the most convenient way to spend. They have a point; it is really convenient to spend. You can spend for an entire month and not worry about it until you reach your max or your bill comes due. Is that such a good thing, though? All joking aside, the truth is that a debit card is just as convenient as a credit card. It works the same way except that the debit card withdraws money from your account immediately. It looks the same, feels the same, and allows you to purchase things the same way.

Safety and Online Safety

What if I lose my debit card or cash? What if a hacker steals my debit card number and drains my account? Won't a credit card protect me from this kind of stuff? Financial safety is a big deal. While debit cards offer protections from theft and online hackers, credit cards are inherently safer because the money is not being drawn directly from your bank account. If your checking account is hacked and you don't have money to pay your other bills, that is obviously a problem. There is a trickle-down effect. Debit card stolen, account drained, temporarily short for the house payment. That scenario is a real possibility and much more of an inconvenience than if the credit card is hacked. If your credit card is hacked, you do not experience a direct negative other than having to get a new card and maybe set up new automatic payments.

The credit card companies have a point here. There is less impact to the consumer if a credit card is stolen or hacked versus a debit card. However, the question you need to ask yourself is how valuable that is to you. Again, it boils down to how responsible you are with paying off your card. If you pay it off each month, this is a very good benefit. However, if you don't pay it off every month, you are paying a very high price in interest and possible late fees for the benefit of added security. Someone paying $300 per month in interest would be hard pressed to make the argument that it's worth it for the added security.

Building Up Your Credit Score

Like it or not, your credit score is going to be looked at for a variety of things. Banks run your credit score if you apply for a home loan, most landlords run your credit if you are applying for an apartment, and some employers will even run your credit when deciding whether or not to hire you. That is a very short list of potential people who may run your credit score. Since your credit score is important, you might as well get it as high as possible. An established track record of paying off a credit card is one of the primary ways to increase your credit score.[9]

The Positives

This section is purposefully short. There are not a lot of benefits to using a credit card, and there is a great deal of risk and things that could go wrong by using a card. People are much more likely to overspend and go into debt than they are to actually benefit from using the card. It is important to acknowledge that there are benefits to credit card use if used appropriately and responsibly 100 percent of the time. The major problem is that the majority of people aren't able to use credit cards in this way. The next section on the negatives to using a credit card is significantly longer and more detailed.

The Negatives

The section on the negatives of using a credit card will be longer than the section on the positives. Why, you ask? Because the negatives far outweigh the positives. Credit card companies are a business. It is a business that has been around for many years, which means they make money. Great money. Possibly your money if you allow it. Credit card companies are exceptionally skilled at offering seemingly great deals, confusing the customer with endless terms and conditions, then taking fees and interest payments for years on end. Credit cards account for billions of dollars in debt in the United States alone. Once someone gets into the spiral of credit card debt, it can take years to get out of it, if at all. According to uscourts.gov, there were approximately 12.8 million consumer bankruptcy petitions filed in US federal courts from 2005–2017, with a high of over $1.5 million in 2010 alone.[10] I'll make a bet that the majority of those bankruptcies involved credit cards in some shape or form.

High Interest Rates and Late Fees

The interest rates on credit cards are outrageous. It is not uncommon for interest rates to hover in the high teens and low twenties. It's not uncommon to see them at 18–24 percent. Think about it, 18–24 percent! That is the credit card company taking your money month after month, year after year. It is a debt deal you are making with the credit card company. Consider this: If you put $4,000 on your credit card and pay just the minimum balance, it will take you almost 11 years to pay off the card—11 years! Here are the numbers: $4,000 at 19 percent interest, paying the minimum of $160 (4 percent of the balance) each month. Doing that will take you almost 11 years. Change the numbers to $5,000 at 19 percent interest, paying off the minimum of $200 (4 percent of balance) each month and it will take you over 11.5 years.

These numbers all assume that you will not be spending any more on the credit card. As those who have ever been in any kind of consumer debt know, that is a highly unrealistic scenario. If you are in a position of having four or five thousand dollars' worth of credit card debt and are only paying the minimum, chances are that you are going to be charging more on the card throughout the subsequent months and years.

The reality is that most people continue to charge more than the minimum payment, which creates an endless cycle of massive debt. Suppose over the course of a year or two you charge the card a couple hundred dollars more than the minimum payments. It doesn't seem like a lot at the time but after a couple years the balance has ballooned up to $8,000. If you pay the minimum each month of $320, it will take you over 13 years to pay off. Again, this is assuming you don't charge another cent to the card, which is a highly unrealistic scenario.

Not only do credit cards charge extraordinarily high interest rates but they also charge late fees. Miss a payment and you will be charged on average a late fee of $36.[11] That's not once a year, that is *every time you are late*. So now you have your original balance, plus high interest rates, plus late fees if applicable. To add to the party, some credit cards even have annual fees.

An Endless Debt Cycle

High interest rates make credit card debt an endless cycle. It's like running in quicksand and giving all your money to the credit card company. Go to work, pay off the credit card. Next month go to work and pay off the credit card again. Those in credit card debt are not getting ahead, they are continually behind. It's a race just to get out of debt and many people are losing this race for years on end.

The cycle is compounded when people carry debt on multiple credit cards, which happens often. All too often, a scenario occurs in which debt is carried on one credit card. The debt compounds and the minimum payments become too large. So the person opens up another credit card to transfer the balance or use the new card for purchases. Then when it's time to pay the second card, it's very difficult. That cycle continues into multiple cards and becomes an almost impossible situation to get out of.

Opportunity Cost of Debt

The concept of opportunity cost is addressed throughout this book. It is especially applicable in relation to carrying credit card debt. The consequences are severe. Using the example from above, if someone is carrying $5,000 worth of credit card debt at 19 percent interest, it will take an astounding 11.5 years to pay off if only paying the minimum. Not only that but over $3,000 of interest will accumulate during that time. That's over $3,000 that could have been invested. With $3,000 invested at 10 percent over a 30-year period, you'd get $52,348!

That is not a typo. That's only with an initial contribution of $3,000. It doesn't even factor in monthly contributions. So those who are carrying credit card debt are not only dealing with being in a constant hole but they are also squandering away the opportunity for compound interest to work in their favor. As Albert Einstein said about compound interest, "He who understands it, earns it. He who doesn't, pays it."[12] How true that is.

Easy to Spend

It's beyond easy to spend money using a credit card. You just pull it out and swipe it or enter a few numbers online. There's no going through your wallet, counting up your $20 bills and handing it to someone. Handing someone cash is painful. Swiping a card isn't. Many financial experts recommend paying for things using all cash because it hurts a lot more to hand it over. This is in stark comparison to using a card. Swiping a card doesn't produce those same uncomfortable feelings. The card is momentarily swiped then you don't see it again until it's time to pay the monthly bill.

---

12 Sam Becker, "Compounding is the Most Powerful Force in the Universe, Einstein Said— This Example Shows Why," *Acorns* (January 22, 2020), https://grow.acorns.com/compounding-penny-doubled/.

Final Verdict

The majority of this chapter addresses the negatives to using a credit card. This is intentional because the negatives outweigh the positives. It is incredibly easy to fall prey to the debt traps that credit card companies create. Credit card companies pump millions into advertisements and marketing campaigns to lure you in as a consumer. Promises of vacations and mounds of "cash back" are placed into consumers' heads so that they will use the card being advertised. Unless you're paying off credit cards every month to where you have zero balance, you are far better off using cash or a debit card.

Action Steps

1. Determine whether or not you want to use a credit card.
2. If you are in credit card debt, make sure the payments are included in your debt payoff plan from Chapter 7.

CHAPTER 9

"Good Debt," and Leveraging Debt

If you want to be rich, you need to know the difference between good debt and bad debt, good expenses, bad expenses, good income and bad income, and good liabilities and bad liabilities.
– Robert Kiyosaki

The concept of "good debt" has been highly debated for years among financial experts, investors, and novices. The first debate is simply if good debt really exists. There are schools of thought that argue any debt is bad. The second debate is what good debt is. Some would say debt is only good when you can leverage it to buy income-producing assets. Others will tell you debt is good if it's used to purchase something that is expected to go up in value over time, such as a house.

Robert Kiyosaki, author of *Rich Dad, Poor Dad*, and many other books, maintains that assets have to produce income for you, including your house. He writes, "Your house is not an asset. It's a liability. Very simply, an asset is something that puts money in your pocket. A liability is something that takes money out of your pocket." So who's right, and what exactly is an asset and what is good debt?

Definition of an Asset

What is an asset and what is a liability? The answer to that specific question will give us the answer to what good debt is. As noted, many "experts" have varying opinions on the topic. To simplify, I will give my definition of an asset. Note: My definition of an asset is catered to the individual, family, and small business, not to corporations (which would change the definition). An asset must meet the following requirements:

1. It's reasonably expected to go up in value over time based on years of data AND you are expecting to hold the asset many years. For example, historical data provided by the National Association of Realtors indicates that home values increased 5.4 percent annually on average from 1968 to 2009. In some years houses may go down in value, and in other years they may have larger gains than normal. The historical averages and your ability or intent to keep the subject investment over many years are the critical factors. Using this definition, a house would be considered an asset but not necessarily an income-producing asset. Note: If an investor is expecting to hold subject property (property on which you have a mortgage) for a short time hoping that it rapidly increases in value, it becomes speculation. While speculation can make people large sums of money in a short amount of time, it does not fit the definition of holding an asset.

2. The subject investment makes money. Examples include cash flowing real estate and a positive cash flow business. For example, suppose you purchase a rental property in an A or B class neighborhood using these numbers:

Purchase Price	$100,000
20% Down Payment	$20,000
Closing Costs	$3,000
Total Down Payment (Including Closing Costs)	$23,000
Monthly Rent	$1,000
Principal and Interest (5.5%)	$454
Insurance	$30
Property Taxes	$100
Property Management	$100
Vacancies Allowance	$50

Repairs Allowance	$70
Capital Expenditures Allowance	$70
Total Monthly Income	$1,000
Total Monthly Expenses	$874
Total Monthly Cash Flow	$126

Using these numbers, the rental property is immediately making the investor $126 per month after expenses are accounted for. This is not a book about finding great real estate deals, so don't look too much into this specific example. It's just a hypothetical rental property used as an example to demonstrate what a cash flowing investment looks like. This is an example of an income-producing asset.

To further clarify what an asset is, criteria number one from above is an example of an asset while criteria number two is an example of an income-producing asset. Both are assets but they have different definitions. Using data, develop your own definition of what an asset is and let that drive your investment decisions. There is a lot of noise out there on the subject, and many of the "experts" won't even entertain the idea that there is more than one answer. This is an area where it's important to gather your own information, establish your own criteria, and invest accordingly.

Leveraging Debt

Now that we have defined what an asset is, we can move on to using "good debt," also known as leveraging debt. Leveraging debt is a strategy used by many investors because it allows the investor to purchase an income producing asset worth much more than what they are paying for it. The rental property cited above is an example of leveraging debt. In this scenario, the investor paid $23,000 out of pocket to purchase an asset appraised at $100,000. The monthly expenses are paid for by the tenant and the investor can make over $100 per month. In other words, an investor can purchase an asset using much less money than it's actually worth. This strategy allows your money to potentially grow more rapidly.

Many investors think of leveraging debt as partnering with the bank. Continuing to use real estate as an example, the investor finds the real estate deal, does all the work involving the property, and the bank provides the upfront capital. Both the investor and bank are assuming risk because they have money invested into the deal. Using the bank as a partner, the investor is able to purchase more rental properties or other income producing investments. The main advantage to this strategy is more income producing assets can be purchased over a shorter amount of time, which allows the properties to collect more rent over the years and experience possible appreciation. Here's an example using three fictitious properties to demonstrate the point, see charts below.

Yearly Appreciation

5.4% yearly appreciation rate*	2009 Value (and purchase price)	2010 Value	2011 Value	2012 Value	2013 Value
000 Main Street	$225,000	$237,150	$249,956	$263,454	$277,681
000 Highland Way	$140,000	$147,560	$155,528	$163,927	$172,779
000 Johnson Avenue	$45,000	$47,430	$49,991	$52,691	$55,536

5.4% yearly appreciation rate*	2014 Value	2015 Value	2016 Value	2017 Value	2018 Value	2019 Value
000 Main Street	$292,676	$308,480	$325,138	$342,695	$361,201	$380,706
000 Highland Way	$182,109	$191,943	$202,308	$213,233	$224,748	$236,884
000 Johnson Avenue	$58,535	$61,696	$65,028	$68,540	$72,241	$76,142

*Historical data provided by the National Association of Realtors indicates that homes increased in value on average 5.4 percent annually from 1968 to 2009.

3 Percent Rent Increases

3% yearly rent increase	2009 Monthly Rent	2010 Monthly Rent	2011 Monthly Rent	2012 Monthly Rent	2013 Monthly Rent
000 Main Street	$2,300	$2,369	$2,440	$2,513	$2,578
000 Highland Way	$1,400	$1,442	$1,485	$1,530	$1,576
000 Johnson Avenue	$650	$670	$690	$711	$732

3% yearly rent increase	2014 Monthly Rent	2015 Monthly Rent	2016 Monthly Rent	2017 Monthly Rent	2018 Monthly Rent
000 Main Street	$2,655	$2,735	$2,817	$2,902	$2,989
000 Highland Way	$1,623	$1,672	$1,722	$1,774	$1,827
000 Johnson Avenue	$754	$777	$800	$824	$849

4 Percent Rent Increases

4% yearly rent increase	2009 Monthly Rent	2010 Monthly Rent	2011 Monthly Rent	2012 Monthly Rent	2013 Monthly Rent
000 Main Street	$2,300	$2,415	$2,535.75	$2,662.54	$2,795.67
000 Highland Way	$1,400	$1,456	$1,500	$1,560	$1,622
000 Johnson Avenue	$650	$676	$703	$731	$760

4% yearly rent increase	2014 Monthly Rent	2015 Monthly Rent	2016 Monthly Rent	2017 Monthly Rent	2018 Monthly Rent
000 Main Street	$2,935.45	$3,082.22	3,236.33	$3,398.15	$3,568.06
000 Highland Way	$1,687	$1,754	$1,824	$1,897	$1,973
000 Johnson Avenue	$790	$822	$855	$889	$925

5 Percent Rent Increases

5% yearly rent increase	2009 Monthly Rent	2010 Monthly Rent	2011 Monthly Rent	2012 Monthly Rent	2013 Monthly Rent
000 Main Street	$2,300	$2,415	$2,535.75	$2,662.54	$2,795.67
000 Highland Way	$1,400	$1,470	$1,544	$1,621	$1,702
000 Johnson Avenue	$650	$683	$717	$753	$791

5% yearly rent increase	2014 Monthly Rent	2015 Monthly Rent	2016 Monthly Rent	2017 Monthly Rent	2018 Monthly Rent
000 Main Street	$2,935.45	$3,082.22	3,236.33	$3,398.15	$3,568.06
000 Highland Way	$1,787	$1,876	$1,970	$2,068	$2,171
000 Johnson Avenue	$831	$873	$917	$963	$1,011

As indicated in the charts, an investor who purchased in 2009 versus 2019 is much better off both in terms of rent and potential appreciation during that time period. While rents are market driven, a 3–5 percent yearly increase during that time period is not unrealistic. While rents do not follow a perfect pattern of increases or decreases, the yearly averages are the metric we will use. Since nobody can predict the future, this is also a metric that many real estate investors use to predict yearly rent increases.

Using 000 Main Street as an example, let's compare the monthly rents in 2009 versus 2018 using a 5 percent rent increase. As shown in the chart, the monthly rent in 2009 was $2,300. In 2018, that same house rented for $3,568.06, an astounding $1,268.06 more in just 10 years' time! That is the power of leveraging debt; the investor was able to purchase the property for a much lower price than it was worth using borrowed money and then got to enjoy both appreciation and rent increases.

By leveraging debt, this investor was also able to purchase more properties during this time period, further increasing her gains and rental portfolio.

This is a much more powerful strategy than just purchasing with cash. In a way, leveraging debt allows you to buy time, and the more time that interest is compounded, the larger it grows on average. The investor in this scenario benefited by thousands of dollars in monthly cash flow and into the hundreds of thousands in equity by leveraging debt and buying time.

There Is Really No Such Thing as Being "Debt Free"

There's really no such thing as being "debt free." I know that is a controversial statement, but I say it because while it is possible to remove and pay off a great majority of debt, there will always be some sort of charges you will owe. Take someone who has paid off their car, house, student loans, and credit cards. That is exceptional, it really is. Anyone who can do that is in great financial position and should be commended. However, this person is not truly debt free. Even with a free and clear house, there are still property taxes, insurance, and maintenance. Ever tried not paying property taxes? The county tax assessor doesn't care if your house is paid off or not. They will foreclose on a paid off house just as fast as a house with a $500,000 mortgage. That fits my definition of debt. Electric and water bills, insurance, internet, among other things, are all forms of monthly debts.

The reason for writing this section is not to encourage you to take out more debt just because nobody is truly debt free and there is no hope. Far from it. The purpose is to encourage you to think critically about your finances. Putting your nose to the grindstone to pay off debt as quickly as possible may not be the best choice for you. For example, if you have a 30-year note on your house for $300,000 at 3.5 percent interest (a rate many people are getting at this time), you may be better off using your money to invest or save for your children's college than rapidly paying off the house ahead of schedule. Even though you are still being charged interest for the life of the loan, there are many arguments to be made for intentionally keeping that debt. Just using one strategy like paying off as much debt as possible without investing is not always the wisest choice. Sure, it feels good to say you are debt free, but what is your overall financial picture?

Being "debt free" is not the holy grail of personal finance, financial freedom is. Brian Buffini made the point in a 2019 podcast that babies are technically born debt free.[13] Those same babies also don't have any assets. You can also have someone with no debt and zero net worth. Is that person really better off than someone with five million in assets and $400,000 in leveraged debt? Of course not. It's critical to look at the *whole financial picture* and be open to utilizing different strategies. Following are three basic reasons to consider leveraging debt.

1. Opportunity Cost

Arguably, the number one reason to consider investing your money instead of pouring it all into paying off your debt faster is opportunity cost. Every extra dollar put into paying off your mortgage faster is a dollar you aren't using to invest. There is a huge opportunity cost there. If your interest rate on the mortgage debt is 3.5 percent and your average rate of return on a potential return on investment is over 8 percent, the simple math says to invest. In this scenario, you already have your house at an excellent interest rate and now also have investments at a high average rate of return.

That's opposed to paying off the debt first and not having the investment producing an 8 percent of return for multiple years. Time in the market is of critical importance in building long-term wealth. I am not suggesting to "get fancy" and start refinancing everything you own to invest; what I am suggesting is to think critically about whether it's better to pay off debt as quickly as possible before investing.

2. Inflation

The average rate of inflation per year since 1913, according to Inflationdata.com, is 3.15 percent. Since a 100 year plus sample size is comprehensive and large enough, let's use that rate. If inflation is occurring at an average of 3.15 percent and assuming you are making more money on a yearly basis, your mortgage debt will naturally become less challenging to pay over the course of a 30-year period. Suppose your monthly payment on the debt is $1,347. As of this writing, $1,347 is worth exactly $1,347. However, as inflation occurs, today's $1,347 will not have the same purchasing power in five years, 10 years, 20 years, etc. The good news is that it also means that your debt will become less expensive if you allow inflation to work for you. The $1,347 you are paying today will be less constraining to pay off in future years. This is where the concept of "inflating out the debt" comes from.

Remember hearing your Great Uncle Jim talk about how an ice cream used to cost only a nickel, how a can of soda cost less than 10 cents, or that they purchased their home for $40,000 and it's now worth 1.5 million? That's inflation at work. You can use inflation as a debt pay-down tool in your own financial strategy simply by letting time take its course. As time passes, as long as the debt is at a fixed rate, it will become easier to pay off. This is, of course, assuming your wages or earned income continue to increase, which historically they do with inflation.

Just because inflation can help you pay off debt does not mean you should take out as much debt as possible. This is where many people get into trouble and why so many financial experts tell you to pay off debt first. Using inflation as a tool needs to be done with caution and should only be used when purchasing actual assets. Pulling $100,000 out of your house to pay for cars and consumer purchases is a sure-fire recipe for financial failure. Inflation or not, that is not a good idea.

3. Tax Benefits

In many cases, mortgage interest for your home and rental properties comes with significant tax advantages. Since I am not a CPA or tax attorney, I am only going to briefly cover this section as an introduction. Talk with a reputable CPA or attorney to learn specific laws and regulations.

Mortgage interest is often tax deductible. (There are other deductions as well, such as property taxes, HOA fees for rentals, depreciation for rentals, etc. Speak with your CPA for more details.) Over the course of a 30-year mortgage, the tax savings add up to a significant amount. If you pay off a tax-deductible note, you are losing that potential for tax savings. Speak with your CPA or tax attorney to strategize the best tax plan for you.

A Critical Warning

The debt strategies addressed in this chapter are to be used with great care. Leveraging debt is to be used with extreme caution and only as a strategy when purchasing income producing assets. That means it is not OK to leverage debt to buy cars, boats, jewelry, etc. To repeat, leveraging debt is only to be used when purchasing income producing assets. Furthermore, if you are going to use this strategy, you need to know what you are doing or work with people who know what they are doing. Again, talk with your CPA or a qualified person for specific strategies.

During the financial crisis beginning in 2007, many real estate investors over-leveraged debt, which left them in the red every month. As the properties lost value, many had to foreclose on their properties. While leveraging debt can provide tremendous gains, it also comes with tremendous risk if used inappropriately or recklessly. During the last recession, many people thought they knew what they were doing but didn't. Speculation in real estate and stocks ran rampant and many people lost a lot of money. People thought they were investing when they were actually speculating.

When deciding whether you want to leverage debt as a strategy, look back to your life and financial goals you wrote about in Chapter 1. Do you want multiple assets that carry debt? Or would having debt cause you too much stress? If carrying debt causes you stress, there is nothing wrong with purchasing one asset at a time using cash and building up your investment portfolio slowly. Whether or not to leverage debt as a strategy depends on the comfort level and expertise of the investor. *Assess your goals and make decisions based on your own goals, not what other people do.* Your goals will guide you on how you want to use debt or not use debt. Remember, optimization is not always the goal; the goal is to develop a sustainable financial strategy that you are comfortable with.

It is always OK to pay off debt as a strategy. No one ever went broke paying off debt. You will not become as wealthy as you could be but if paying off debt helps you sleep at night and gives you security, that is a perfectly acceptable strategy.

Action Step

Write down all your good debt. Decide if you want to keep it or pay it off.

CHAPTER 10

The Silent Killers: Financing Luxury Items and Spending Money While at Work

A fool and his money are soon parted.
– Thomas Tusser

Americans love toys. We love having the fanciest car, the newest gadget, and the nicest boat. For years, these items have been a symbol of success. We see someone driving a brand-new truck towing a $30,000 boat and assume that person is rich and successful. We assume he or she has a high paying job, a nice house, and great family and friends. They go out to eat at expensive restaurants every day at work and always seem to be carrying around a cup of coffee around the office from the trendiest coffee shops. They've got it all, right?

Not necessarily, the data says. A study by NerdWallet done in December 2018 found the average American household carries almost $7,000 in credit card debt and more than $28,000 in car loans.[14] That doesn't even include student loans or mortgage balances. That guy driving the new truck towing the expensive boat more than likely does not own either item. If you must, luxury items should be purchased in cash and enjoyed for personal reasons, not to impress others.

Silent Killer #1: Financing Luxury Items

People love to show off their stuff and appear successful. If the banks or credit cards will lend it to us, we buy it—and keep buying until the banks say no or we reach our credit limits. Over time, the financing of luxury items adds up to tremendous costs and puts us in a hole almost impossible to dig out of. The interest and minimum payments alone often become unpayable. We barely notice that it's happening behind the curtain of all our nice things. Before long, it's too late, and the debt becomes overwhelming. It sounds blatantly obvious, but remember, it's fast and easy to get into debt but very hard to get out of. Let's look at two examples of fictional couples in situations that happen all the time in real life.

John and Marie

John and Marie locked eyes at a Halloween party their senior year of college, and the rest is history. Before too long they have two kids, a Golden Retriever, two brand new cars, and a boat in the garage. They both make over $120,000 per year for a combined income of almost $250,000. The neighborhood they live in is filled with custom built homes with golf course views. John and Marie seem to have it all. Now both 35, John and Marie enjoy their lifestyle and living in their nice neighborhood, but things have not been so great the past three years. The boat cost more than John wanted to pay, but his buddy Kevin had the newest model, so John didn't want to look cheap. He went ahead and paid the extra $4,500 for the newest model.

Both cars were bought brand new and almost completely financed. Marie's sedan cost $42,000 and John's truck was just shy of $40,000. The new car payments made things tighter, which meant they didn't always pay off the credit cards. Most months, John and Marie were able to pay only the minimum balance on their multiple credit cards. The bills were starting to add up and it was causing great stress in the marriage. Marie felt like John was always nagging her about money when the truth was he spent just as much as she did. John felt like Marie didn't understand, or didn't want to understand, his concerns about money or anything else anymore. They started avoiding money conversations altogether but the bills kept adding up. They still owed $75,000 on the cars, had $675,000 left on the house, and $32,000 in credit card debt. Both John and Marie were highly stressed and felt like they were trapped.

Tina and Nick

Tina and Nick live about five minutes from John and Marie, but their story is much different. Tina and Nick make $135,000 (pre-tax) combined, much less than John and Marie, but they *always have a monthly surplus*. They just purchased a rental home that makes them an additional $200 per month. Tina and Nick aren't sure if they want to buy more rental homes, but they enjoy collecting a monthly check while their property manager handles all the calls from tenants.

A few years back, Tina and Nick decided they were tired of living paycheck to paycheck. They read a few books about personal finance and decided that what really made them happy was time with family. They sold the expensive car and replaced it with a reliable four door. They sold the camping trailer they only used twice per year, ridding themselves of the $275 monthly payment. Tina and Nick came to the conclusion that many of the large expenses they had accumulated were not adding value or joy to their lives.

Tina and Nick also began to automate their savings, paying themselves first. While the money didn't seem to accumulate very quickly, within a year and a half, Tina and Nick noticed a substantial increase in their net worth. They no longer live paycheck to paycheck and both are much less stressed at work and at home. Tina calculated that they are now saving a little over $3,300 per month. She projected that number will move to over $4,000 a month within three years, after her and Nick get a couple of raises, all of which will be automated into their savings and investment plan.

Life has never been better for Tina and Nick. They are enjoying the freedom of not having to live paycheck to paycheck and are very optimistic about their financial future. They find their financial plan to be sustainable and easy to follow. Tina and Nick cite three things in no particular order as the biggest reasons to their financial success.

1. Selling the expensive car.
2. Automating their savings.
3. Aligning their spending with their values.

Monthly Income for John and Marie and Tina and Nick

	Monthly Income After Taxes	Monthly Expenses	Monthly Passive Investment Income	Total Monthly Savings & Investments
John and Marie	$14,000	$14,000+	N/A	$0
Tina and Nick	$7,875	$4,575	$200	$3,500

As the comparison of these two couples illustrates, financing items on credit cards, massive car payments, and other consumer debt comes with a tremendous cost. Even though John and Marie make a considerable amount more than Tina and Nick, they are not able to get ahead on their bills. Getting ahead in your finances requires more than just a high income. People often find that luxury items don't make them happy, they actually do the opposite by creating additional stress with the high payments they are creating. It takes work, strategy, and education to be financially successful. Just going to work, grinding away, and then spending frivolously will not get the job done.

This portion of the book is not meant to be a knock on buying nice things or encourage a scarcity mindset. Rather, it's meant to show the true cost of purchasing luxury items. As you assess what's important, you may decide that owning a luxury car or boat is important to you. There is nothing wrong with that. Just make sure all your purchases are well thought out, align with your values, and that you are being intentional with your money. Remember, for every dollar spent on a luxury item, that is one less dollar you can invest. And for every dollar financed to purchase a luxury item, the real dollar amount is much greater after factoring in interest and additional opportunity cost.

Silent Killer #2: Spending Money at Work

Spending money at work is the second silent killer of personal finance. Financially speaking, the primary purpose of going to work is to make money, not to spend money. *Spending money while at work is an immediate, self-inflicted pay cut.* Additionally, spending money at work is completely avoidable with a small amount of planning and intentionality. The good news in all of this is that you are in complete control of whether you spend money at work or not. So whether you are already on top of it and spend little to nothing while at work, or spend a lot of money at work, you are in control.

The Self-Inflicted Pay Cut

Suppose nursing assistant Norman makes $20 an hour after taxes. He spends $3 at the coffee kiosk in the morning and another $3 in the afternoon. He also buys lunch at the cafeteria for $7. Additionally, Norman frequents the vending machines at least once a day for a beverage or afternoon snack, costing right around $2. Norman typically spends on average at least $15 per day.

Norman works eight-hour shifts. At $20 per hour after taxes, he makes $160 per day. However, after adjusting for everything he buys while at work, Norman actually makes $145 per day. Assuming Norman works five days per week, this habit of buying snacks and lunch at work costs Norman $75 per week and almost $4,000 for the year. If Norman brings his own lunch, snacks, and coffee to work it would cost him about $3 per day, $15 for the week, and $780 for the year. So Norman is paying over $3,000 per year for the convenience of not having to prepare his own food and drinks. That's an incredibly high tax for a small convenience. Not to mention that Norman doesn't even realize what he is doing. It has become a habit for him to spend at work and he has no idea what it really costs him.

A little bit of planning goes a long way. Not to keep picking on Norman but there's a lot to unpack with him. If Norman had simply planned out his meals and avoided spending money at work, he would have $3,000 a year more in his pocket. That's just in one year. And $3,000 invested yearly at a 10 percent rate of return adds up to $542,380 over a 30-year period. That is not a misprint, spending money at work is costing Norman $542,380! This is a tremendous cost just for a minor convenience.

The reality for people like Norman is that they probably aren't even thinking about what they are doing. It's second nature to purchase food and drink at work; it all seems perfectly normal. If you told someone like Norman that they could simply bring their lunch to work and accumulate over half a million dollars in 30 years, they would probably start to change their habits. It's doubtful that a guy like Norman enjoys vending machine food any more than he would a lunch he brought in himself. That's where the education piece comes in. You don't know what you don't know, so it's important to educate yourself on certain financial principles to optimize your financial situation. Education creates opportunity and choices that you never knew existed.

You Can Still Socialize!

Some would argue that going out and getting food at work is a nice break and a good time to socialize with coworkers. You can still go out with co-workers and socialize! You just aren't spending all the money on food like you used to. For example, if you used to go out to the coffee cart during the morning break with a few friends, you can still walk down with them. The only difference is you are carrying your coffee thermos with you while they pay for their coffee. The walk is the same, the socialization is the same, and the break is the same. You are still having your socialization needs met while saving money. I'll even bet that a few of your friends will take notice and ask you about it. When they find out the true cost of what they are doing, they may join you in bringing in their own coffee thermos.

To clarify, if you really enjoy the coffee or snack and value it, keep ordering it. If the coffee kiosk at work makes the absolute best coffee in the world and you just have to have it every day, go for it. Or if the muffins at the corner store are unlike anything in the world and it makes your day that much better, go ahead with it. Just make sure you are being intentional and realize the cost associated with the daily purchase. What you really want to avoid is mindless spending.

Fast Food and Convenience Stores

Spending money at work is not just limited to vending machines, food trucks, and coffee kiosks. It also includes leaving work and driving to convenience stores and drive-through fast food. So many people on their way to work stop at the convenience store for a coffee and breakfast. People do it without thinking, and the costs and negative health effects add up over time. The same thing goes for lunch breaks and after work. So many people without thinking stop for fast food or little snacks and beverages at convenience stores throughout the day. Not only are these extremely unhealthy habits, they will also put tremendous financial strain on your wallet.

Years ago, I worked with someone who constantly complained about his financial position. It was hard for him to pay the rent, and he said he had no money saved. He blamed it on the economy and the "rich people" taking it all. However, without fail, this same guy came into work every single morning with a large coffee and pastry. He would then get fast food for lunch. Conservatively, this man's eating habits at work cost him well over $10 a day, probably closer to $15, yet every day he continued to arrive with his coffee and pastry in hand and complained about not having money.

Be Intentional

The key to avoiding spending at work, just like in other areas, is being intentional. There is nothing wrong with getting the occasional cup of coffee or grabbing lunch with work friends every now and then. Meeting over lunch with clients or associates is probably something you don't want to miss either. Business often gets done at lunch, so don't ignore potential opportunities just to save a few bucks.

Just make sure it aligns with your values and it's something you want to do, either for personal or for professional reasons. In the case of a business lunch, use common sense to determine if you should go or not. For example, if the owner of a successful business invites you to lunch to discuss a new position in the company, it would be very unwise to refuse that offer just to avoid spending the money. The amount of money you could eventually see by attending the meeting far outweighs the cost.

Go back to your goals and values, they probably don't align with spending large amounts of money while at work. For example, if your goal is to invest $12,000 per year in index funds, spending hundreds, if not thousands of dollars at work on a yearly basis probably doesn't align with that goal. In this example, those daily cups of coffee hold you back from your big goals. Don't let slight conveniences or lack of knowledge hold you back anymore. Be aware of this spending issue and take the necessary action steps to rectify the situation to your satisfaction.

Action Steps

1. Eliminate at least one unnecessary expense at work.
2. If you are currently financing a luxury item and feel stressed about the payments, consider selling it.

CHAPTER 11

Cars: The Shocking Cost and the Myth of Car Loans

I'm not against people having new cars. I'm against them having you. We spend a tremendous amount impressing somebody at the stoplight who we'll never meet. It makes you broke and keeps you broke.
– Dave Ramsey

Cars. They almost seem like a basic need. It would be unfathomable not to have a car for many people. Sure, public transportation is OK now and then, but cars are where it's at, especially if you don't live in a big city. Cars offer unmatched convenience and reliability compared to other forms of transportation. People use their cars for business, pleasure, taking the family out to dinner, among a myriad other things. Cargroup.org reports that automobile sales contribute between 3–3.5 percent to the overall gross domestic product (GDP).[15] Automobile companies know this so they pour in millions of dollars each year in advertising. Cars are a huge part of American's daily lives and the overall economy. It wouldn't be outlandish to say that cars are engrained in American culture.

The American Dream

It is frequently said that the American dream is to purchase a home. However, before that comes to dream to start driving and own a car. It is almost a rite of passage for a 16-year-old to begin driving and eventually get their own set of wheels. Cars represent the end of an era for families; the kid starts driving and all of a sudden they don't need a ride to school or social events. They can even drive themselves on dates (not covered in this book!).

In many cases, the teenager even gets their own car. Cars are portrayed to represent freedom, independence, and even luxury. The open road of life, all starting behind the wheel.

As a disclaimer, both my wife and I own a car. We have two cars for the family, which allows us to be more efficient with our time. We live in an area without great public transportation and cars allow us to minimize our transportation time. Cars are a major convenience for our family. However, this convenience comes with a significant cost. By making the choice to own two cars, we are paying dearly for it. The costs of automobile ownership are in a word, shocking.

The Shocking Cost of Automobiles

Most families own two cars.[16] Now let's take a look at the real costs of an automobile purchase. The data below is calculated from Edmunds.com "Cost to Own Calculator."[17] As an example, let's look at a very popular 2019 SUV. We will assume it is driven 15,000 miles annually for five years, has a purchase price of $35,536 with 10 percent down, and it is purchased new.

	Year 1	Year 2	Year 3	Year 4	Year 5	Total
Tax Credit	$0	$0	$0	$0	$0	$0
Insurance	$1,310	$1,356	$1,403	$1,452	$1,503	$7,024
Maintenance	$298	$888	$441	$2,239	$947	$4,813
Repairs	$0	$0	$152	$362	$529	$1,043
Taxes and Fees	$3,135	$236	$221	$207	$191	$3,990
Financing Interest	$1,911	$1,537	$1,138	$712	$257	$5,555
Depreciation	$8,749	$2,268	$2,147	$2,518	$2,384	$18,066
Fuel	$3,024	$3,115	$3,208	$3,304	$3,403	$16,054
Cost to Own	$18,427	$9,400	$8,710	$10,794	$9,214	$56,545

This vehicle costs $56,545 over a five-year period! That number is truly astounding. Just for the heck of it, ask a few of your friends in the next few days what they think it costs to own a car like this. I'll bet they are not even close and that they will be shocked when you tell them. We truly don't have an idea of what cars cost. When it comes to cars, we just kind of go along with the herd without thinking about it.

What if we decided to purchase a slightly used four door sedan instead? We'll use a common four door sedan, 2016 model for this example.

	Year 1	Year 2	Year 3	Year 4	Year 5	Total
Tax Credit	$0	$0	$0	$0	$0	$0
Insurance	$1,309	$1,348	$1,389	$1,430	$1,473	$6,949
Maintenance	$329	$1,730	$755	$1,124	$1,352	$5,290
Repairs	$250	$367	$427	$500	$583	$2,127
Taxes and Fees	$1,299	$141	$132	$124	$117	$1,813
Financing Interest	$812	$653	$484	$302	$109	$2,360
Depreciation	$2,759	$1,354	$1,192	$1,056	$948	$7,309
Fuel	$1,557	$1,604	$1,652	$1,702	$1,753	$8,268
Cost to Own	$8,315	$7,197	$6,031	$6,238	$6,335	$34,116

It costs $34,416 over a five-year period, which is about $22,429 less than the SUV. Although $34,416 is still a lot of money, it is significantly less than what the SUV cost over the same time period. If $22,429 were to be invested over a 30-year period, you would end up with $391,373. That's just for purchasing a used four door sedan over a new SUV. This is called opportunity cost, which we will go greater into detail later this chapter. Let's break down some of the reasons why cars are so expensive.

Insurance

Car insurance is expensive. The insurance providers are taking a risk by insuring you so they charge a hefty premium. The average yearly cost of insurance for the two cars in our example is over $1,300, according to Edmunds' "Cost of Car Ownership" calculator. Shop around for different insurance providers to find the best rates. If you use the same provider for your car and house, you may be able to bundle rates as well. As your car gets older, talk with your agent about dropping certain aspects of the coverage. For example, if you have a 15-year-old car worth less than $2,000, you may not need the same level of insurance as you would for a car worth $15,000.

Maintenance

Not to be confused with repairs, maintenance is the routine work that needs to be done on your car to keep it running at an optimal level. Maintenance is an often forgotten about piece of car ownership that comes with high costs. Maintenance has to be factored into the cost of owning any car and is not something that can be ignored or costly problems arise later. Examples include oil changes, tune ups, tire rotation, and replacing spark plugs.

Repairs

Repairs differ from maintenance in that repairs are fixing something that is broken. If certain repairs are not completed, the car will not run. There is usually a sense of urgency about repairs and they are often considered an emergency. If you have an emergency account set up, you will have money to take care of repairs. If you don't, it can become a financial crisis.

Taxes and Fees

The sticker price of a car is not just the cost of a car. There are always taxes and fees attached. Taxes are a major item that people forget about when purchasing a car. The more expensive the car is, the higher the taxes will be. So a $50,000 car will have more taxes than a $10,000 car. In California, where I live, sales tax is 7.25 percent. If I purchase a car for $50,000, the tax will be $3,625. A car purchased for $10,000 will have a sales tax of $725. Clearly the less expensive car has lower sales tax. However, that's not the end of taxes and fees. Every year you will need to pay more in taxes and fees in the form of car registration. In our example using the SUV, registration in year two is $236 and $221 the following year. Taxes and fees continue to be collected every year you own and drive the car.

Financing Interest

This is a huge category that you have a lot of control over. The interest from financing to purchase a car is incredibly expensive. For the SUV, the interest paid in year one was $1,911. In year two, you paid $1,537. This goes on for five years, totaling an astounding $5,555. That's right, *$5,555 in interest*. You will receive no tax benefit from this, no money back on part of the interest, and no credits from the car dealership. This is just money you are taking out of your pocket and giving to the bank so they can invest it and make even more money.

Pay Cash for Cars

If you are going to buy a car, pay cash for it. Paying cash for cars completely eliminates any financing interest. That money stays in your pocket where it belongs. There is absolutely no reason to pay the bank interest payments when you could be paying cash.

Paying cash for cars offers a secondary benefit that not many people talk about. It is very painful to save up money and then hand it over to the car dealership or private party in exchange for a car. You've worked hard for that money and saved up for some time. Because of this uncomfortable feeling, natural human behavior is to try and find a car that costs less or to hold onto your existing car. This instinct will save you tremendous money over time; allow your instincts to help you.

Let's use an example of someone who has saved up $12,000 for a car. She's got the money and is able to make the purchase whenever she finds the right car. Suppose it took five years for her to save up the $12,000. She is much more likely to try and find a great deal so that she can keep some of the money she saved. Or if she is going to spend the entire $12,000, she is going to make sure she is getting a car worth that money. She's going to make sure the car was checked out by a mechanic, she's going to read the reports on the car, and actively comparison shop.

The mindset of a person buying a car with cash is much different from someone using financing. It's future money and doesn't seem real. The payments seem manageable when broken down into monthly payments. The harsh reality though is that "future money" will end up costing a lot more in interest and opportunity cost than if the money was just saved up.

Depreciation

You may have heard that as soon as anyone drives a new car off the lot, they are immediately losing value on the car. How much value? According to the Edmunds "Cost of Car Ownership" calculator, a new SUV purchased for $35,536 loses $8,749 in year one alone. In year two, an additional $2,268 is lost in depreciation. After five short years, $18,066 is lost in depreciation. Think about that number: $18,066. That's just for driving the car off the lot and using it for five years.

Used Versus New

Buying a car used instead of new helps significantly with depreciation. Although you will continue to lose money every year you own a car, purchasing used avoids the big hit that new car owners experience the moment they drive the car off the lot. Depending on the make and model of the vehicle, a car typically will lose around 10 percent of its value in the first month after driving it off the lot, according to a report from Carfax.[18] So if a new car costs $50,000, it loses $5,000 in the first month after driving it off the lot. A new $40,000 car loses $4,000. A $30,000 car would lose $3,000 and so on down the line. Purchasing used avoids this initial big hit. Purchasing a used car that is a few years old avoids even more depreciation but obviously comes with the risks associated with an older car.

Fuel

Another hidden cost of owning a vehicle is fuel costs. Unless you own an electric car, which are becoming more and more common, you will be paying high costs in fuel. Nonelectric cars need fuel to run, there is no getting around it. Be aware of this cost when purchasing a car. Obviously, the better the gas mileage, the less fuel costs you will incur. Fuel cost estimates should be factored in *before* purchasing a car. Let's make a side by side comparison of the two cars we have been using as examples in this chapter.

	Year 1	Year 2	Year 3	Year 4	Year 5	Total
Fuel-SUV	$3,024	$3,115	$3,208	$3,304	$3,403	$16,054
Fuel-Four Door Sedan	$1,557	$1,604	$1,652	$1,702	$1,753	$8,268
Difference	$1,467	$1,511	$1,556	$1,602	$1,650	$7,786

Yet again, the numbers are significant: $7,786 more in fuel costs alone! That is just to purchase the SUV versus the four door sedan.

Benefits You Are Not Getting

For personal car use, there is no tax credit on any of the money you put into the car unless you use it for business. Talk with your CPA about specific write offs. The reality is most people will get zero tax credit for their vehicles.

Cars Are NOT an Asset

Contrary to what the car companies tell you, your car is not an asset. Assets

---

18   Charles Krome, "Car Depreciation: How Much Value Will a New Car Lose?" Carfax, (November 9, 2018), https://www.carfax.com/blog/car-depreciation.

make money or are expected to go up in value over time. Cars depreciate in value and cost you a lot of money each month to own. That's the exact opposite of an asset. Cars get you from point A to point B and are convenient to use. They take you to and from work, where you can make money. Cars can take you and your family on awesome vacations. There are a lot of good things about cars but they are not an asset. Cars cost you money every month.

Step onto a used car lot and within a couple minutes, you will hear words and phrases from the salesperson like "investment," "wise choice," "last for years," and so on. Cars are there to get you reliably and comfortably from place to place, and anything more than that is a luxury and an extra cost. Leather seats, 18-inch rims, seat warmers, and the "premium package" are all luxuries. It's OK to purchase luxuries, just be aware and intentional about what you are buying. Do not confuse a car purchase with investing or purchasing an asset.

Opportunity Cost: The Biggest Killer

Opportunity cost is one of the least talked about parts of owning a car but perhaps the costliest. When money is spent on something like a car or motorcycle, it cannot be invested. It's a very simple concept. If you spend $30,000 on a car, that same $30,000 cannot be invested in an asset. In this section, we will analyze the opportunity costs for each part of car ownership: insurance, maintenance, repairs, taxes and fees, financing (for many), depreciation, and fuel.

The three most important elements of car ownership to focus on are financing, depreciation, and fuel costs. Typically, these three areas are the costliest. The good news is that these are also the three areas we have the most control over. When purchasing a car, it is critical to carefully analyze these three costs especially. Making the right decision in even one of these areas can literally lead to hundreds of thousands of dollars extra over 30 years. Therefore, we will spend more time in each of these sections versus the other elements of car ownership. The tables below refer to our SUV example.

Opportunity Cost of Insurance

The total paid for insurance over a five-year period is $7,024. The opportunity cost, if invested over a 30-year period, earning 10 percent.

Start	Year 1	Year 5	Year 10	Year 20	Year 30
$7,024	$7,726	$11,312	$18,218	$47,254	$122,565

Opportunity Cost of Maintenance

The total paid in maintenance over a five-year period is $4,813. The opportunity cost, if invested over a 30-year period, earning 10 percent.

Start	Year 1	Year 5	Year 10	Year 20	Year 30
$4,813	$5,294	$7,751	$12,484	$32,379	$83,984

Opportunity Cost of Repairs

The total paid for repairs over a five-year period is $1,043. The opportunity cost, if invested over a 30-year period, earning 10 percent.

Start	Year 1	Year 5	Year 10	Year 20	Year 30
$1,043	$1,147	$1,680	$2,705	$7,017	$18,200

Opportunity Cost of Taxes and Fees

The total taxes and fees paid over a five-year period are $3,990. The opportunity cost, if invested over a 30-year period, earning 10 percent.

Start	Year 1	Year 5	Year 10	Year 20	Year 30
$3,990	$4,389	$6,426	$10,349	$26,843	$69,623

Opportunity Cost of Financing Cars

The total financing interest paid over a five-year period is $5,555. The opportunity cost, if invested over a 30-year period, earning 10 percent.

Start	Year 1	Year 5	Year 10	Year 20	Year 30
$5,555	$6,111	$8,946	$14,408	$37,371	$96,931

The $96,931 in year 30 is not a misprint. That money you paid in interest to the bank could have turned into almost $100,000 for you over a 30-year period. Instead it was given to the bank, who invested it themselves and made almost $100,000 of what should have been your money.

Banks make money when we pay interest. That's interest that we should be earning ourselves. Understand that if you are doing this, you are taking away your wealth and helping the bank get richer. Car payments are not just a set amount of money you give to the bank each month. Each dollar you spend on interest for a car payment is opportunity cost dollars that could have been making you wealthy. However, it's ultimately your choice. You can keep financing cars and make the banks rich or start paying for cars with cash so you can start making yourself rich.

Opportunity Cost of Depreciation

In general, the more money spent upfront on a new or newer car, the more you will lose in depreciation on that purchase. The more you lose in depreciation, the less money you have to invest. Therefore, the opportunity cost is incredibly significant. Buying an expensive new car is very costly. Using our SUV example, the depreciation costs equal $18,066 over a five-year period. Let's take a look at the opportunity cost of this money, assuming the money is earning 10 percent interest.

The total depreciation costs over a five-year period equal $18,066. The opportunity cost, if invested over a 30-year period, earning 10 percent.

Start	Year 1	Year 5	Year 10	Year 20	Year 30
$18,066	$19,873	$29,095	$46,859	$121,539	$315,241

Over a 30-year period, depreciation will end up costing you $315,241. Purchasing a new car seems fairly benign, but when looking at the consequences over a 30-year period, the costs are astronomical. Fortunately, this is one of the areas you have tremendous control over. The simple choice of purchasing a vehicle a few years older at a reasonable price instead of a new and expensive car can make you exponentially wealthier. To greater compound your savings, hold onto the car longer than five years.

Each year you hold the car, the less it is worth. That is both good and bad. It's bad if you try and resell your car because you will get less money than if you had sold it a few years before. However, the good news is that the longer you hold onto your car, the less you will lose in depreciation, especially as you get over the three-year mark. Suppose you purchased a car 12 years ago for $30,000. Let's assume a depreciation rate of 17 percent per year.

$30,000 Purchase Price	Year 1	Year 2	Year 3	Year 4	Year 5
Yearly Depreciation Amount	$5,100	$4,233	$3,513	$2,916	$2,420

Year 6	Year 7	Year 8	Year 9	Year 10	Year 11	Year 12
$2,009	$1,667	$1,384	$1,149	$953	$791	$657

By year 12, you are only losing $657 in depreciation per year. That is in contrast to the first year when you lost $5,100. The longer you can keep your car, the less you will lose in depreciation. You have a lot of control in this area simply by keeping your car. Of course, this comes with the caveat that you have kept your car in good working order and the car continues to be reliable. If all of those factors are not met, the car could actually end up costing you more to own due to repairs and maintenance. You'll have to run the numbers to see what makes the most sense if you own a car that is over 10 years old.

Opportunity Cost of Fuel

Fuel efficiency is another area that you have great control over when purchasing a vehicle. You can find out the fuel costs and miles per gallon for any car online before you buy it. The more fuel efficient a vehicle is, the less you spend. The less you spend in fuel, the more you have to invest. This is where opportunity cost again comes into play. Our SUV is estimated to cost $16,054 in fuel over a five-year period. The opportunity cost, if invested over a 30-year period, earning 10 percent.

Start	Year 1	Year 5	Year 10	Year 20	Year 30
$16,054	$17,659	$25,855	$41,640	$108,033	$280,133

The $280,133 over a 30-year period seems like a lot of money because it is a lot of money. Fuel costs over a five-year period for this particular SUV cost us almost $300,000 in opportunity cost over a 30-year period. Purchasing a more fuel-efficient car puts the money back into your pocket where you can invest it into assets that make you money instead of giving it to the oil companies. Suppose that instead of purchasing the SUV, you purchased our other example vehicle, the midsize four-door sedan. Over a five-year period, making this simple choice would save you $7,786 in fuel costs alone. If we invested this amount over a 30-year period at 10 percent, the total fuel costs saved over a five-year period if purchasing a four-door sedan instead of an SUV are $7,786. The opportunity cost, if invested over a 30-year period, earning 10 percent.

Start	Year 1	Year 5	Year 10	Year 20	Year 30
$7,786	$8,565	$12,539	$20,195	$52,380	$135,861

Simply purchasing a four-door sedan with better gas mileage and investing the difference of $7,786 at a 10 percent return will yield over $135,000 over a 30-year period. That's without having to add any additional money; we're just talking about the money saved from the reduced fuel costs. It's not rocket science and it's not difficult to do, it is just a matter of doing it.

Again, this is a book primarily about creating a new financial mindset and providing information to help make more optimal financial decisions. This book isn't designed to tell you to buy one car over another, it's just providing information to help you make informed decisions. Your family situation might be one in which you have four kids and need a larger car to go anywhere together. In that case, you may decide to have one large car, such as an SUV, and one smaller car for commuting to work. It's your decision; it's just important to have all the information so you can make an informed decision.

One Car Per Family, and Not Owning a Vehicle

In this section, let's address the unthinkable: Having one car per family and then going to the extreme of not owning a car at all. I know, I know, what would your friends think of you. But what if you could optimize your vehicle costs by cutting them in half or not having any vehicle costs at all? It seems impossible, right? It's actually worked for a growing number of individuals and families. Let's take a look at the numbers, first for a household with two cars and drop it down to one. For our example, we will use the SUV so we can have an apples to apples comparison. If a family of four with two SUVs and two drivers were to sell one of their SUVs, they would save approximately $56,545 over a five-year period.

	Year 1	Year 2	Year 3	Year 4	Year 5	Total
Cost to Own	$18,427	$9,400	$8,710	$10,794	$9,214	$56,545

If this same family turned around and invested the $56,545 over a 30-year period at a 10 percent return, it would look like this:

Start	Year 1	Year 5	Year 10	Year 20	Year 30
$56,545	$62,200	$91,066	$146,663	$380,406	$986,676

That's right, over a 30-year period, this family of four would accumulate almost one million dollars just by having one car for a five-year period of time. Many people mistake the cost of owning a car as just the original cost. However, as you can see, it is so much more. Just out of curiosity, how would a family benefit financially by getting rid of both SUVs and having no car?

Start	Year 1	Year 5
$56,545(2)=$113,090	$124,399	$182,133

Year 10	Year 20	Year 30
$293,326	$760,813	$1,973,353

If our subject family were to invest the money instead of purchasing any SUVs, they would accumulate almost two million dollars over a 30-year period! It almost seems impossible that just two cars over a five-year period could end up being worth so much. Yet it's true, and furthermore, millions of people around the world do not recognize this truth. Granted, it may not be realistic for you or your family to get by without having at least one vehicle, especially if you live in a more rural area. But what if you could find a way to just have one car for you and your family?

Is there a way for you to eliminate one car? Could one spouse drop off the other at work? Can one person take public transportation, carpool, bike, or walk to work? Or if you're single, can a roommate or friend take you to the store to get groceries when you need them, and take the train or walk to work? Can one person work from home? Again, the answers to all these questions may be no but with the extreme financial consequence, isn't it worth exploring? Especially if you live in a city or a dense area, there may be several options to have only one car or even no cars. Some people living in more dense areas even discover that the only reason they still have a car is that they just never thought about not having one. Everyone else has a car, so why not have one too? Just kind of seemed like the normal thing to do. No one is asking you to bike 30 miles in the snow, but is it possible that there may be a reasonable method you haven't thought of before?

Summary

Cars are incredibly expensive. Not just in the purchase cost but in the maintenance, depreciation, insurance, and fuel. And most importantly, in the opportunity cost. A car seems innocent enough. Buy it and it's yours, right? There is so much more to cars than meets the eye. Cars are full of hidden costs and opportunity costs that not only keep people in debt but also keep them from investing. Cars are more than the sticker price. And the more expensive a car is, the more it is costing you in both direct costs and opportunity costs.

My hope with this chapter is that it shows just how costly cars really are. Buying an expensive car can literally keep you from achieving great wealth later in life. It is shocking to see the real numbers; just one vehicle's costs over a five-year period can end up costing you in upwards of one million dollars.

Action Steps

1. Find at least two ways you can reduce car costs. Implement those steps immediately.
2. Take five minutes to just think about the possibility of having one car or no cars.

CHAPTER 12

Intentional Shopping

If you buy things you don't need, soon you will have to sell things you need.
– Warren Buffett

A myth that has carried on for generations is that you must cut coupons and actively seek to find deals to save money at the store. We all have a picture in our heads of a person sitting at the table diligently cutting coupons for hours on end or endlessly scouring the internet just to save a few bucks. While some may enjoy finding sales, you can save money at the store by just being a smart shopper. This takes almost no effort or extra time, just a little common sense and awareness. You don't have to spend 10 hours a week finding online coupons to save $10 at the grocery store. A simple tweak of spending habits at the grocery store can save significant money while costing almost nothing time wise. Remember, we want to be as efficient as possible with our time and finances. Spending endless hours trying to save a few dollars really isn't worth our time.

The Staples

Think about what food you eat on a regular basis, the staples of your diet. What household items do you consistently use? Cereal, mustard, granola bars, paper towels, toilet paper, soap. These are all items you can buy in bulk for less money and store at your home for long periods of time. It is much more cost effective to purchase these items in bulk than to purchase in small quantities at a traditional grocery store, or worse, at a convenience store. Buying in bulk also helps you avoid taking additional trips to the store.

What food and other kinds of items do you regularly purchase that can't be found at a bulk store? Specialty snacks, toiletries, certain lunch meats, fruits, etc. Make an effort to purchase more of these specific items when they are on sale. For example, suppose you only use a certain brand of face wipes because of a sensitive skin issue. If you happen to be at the store and see that brand on sale, purchase more than you normally would. Let's say they normally cost $3.99 a pack but you find them on sale for $2.99 a pack, buy five packs for a quick savings of $5 and you won't have to buy them again for a few months. No coupons or massive amounts of effort and energy needed, just common sense. That is a quick and easy $5 dollars saved with almost zero effort. That money is not going to change your life but following this principle will.

The same principle applies to food. For example, take a certain protein bar you eat before or after the gym that you can't find at the bulk store. They normally cost $5 for a pack of 10. You are already at the store and happen to see them on sale for $3.75 for a pack of 10. Buy five packs and save an easy $6.25. Almost no extra thought or time required, just a commonsense approach, and eventually it will be habit forming. The only reason people don't do this is that they don't think to do it. Start training your mind to think in this way so you can take advantage of really easy savings with almost no effort. Think of it as free cash.

Food and Brand Alternatives

Some foods and products may be nonnegotiable for you. Using the example above with the face wipes, your dermatologist has recommended just three brands due to your sensitive skin. You tried all three but only ABC Skincare keeps you from breaking out. There's not a lot of wiggle room there; it's not worth switching to another brand at the expense of your skin care, appearance, and comfort to save money. Take a look at other items you regularly use though. Suppose you like to eat a certain brand of snack in the afternoon. Is there another brand of the same snack that is less costly? Maybe your preferred snack brand costs $3.25 a pack but another brand costs $2.75. You realize you can't even tell the difference so why not buy the less expensive brand? That's a savings of 50 cents four times a month, adding up to two dollars a month.

Two dollars a month won't make one bit of difference in your financial picture, you say. And I completely agree with that statement! What does make a difference is consistently being mindful and intentional with your money at the store and finding deals without sacrificing quality or time. Training yourself to shop smart over time equals big results. Developing positive financial habits will compound over time. Using just our examples above, we saved $5 on face wipes, $6.25 on protein bars, and $2 by switching snack brands. That's $13.25 for the month on just three products. Again, that amount of money is not going to make or break you, but following these principles monthly will add up to significant savings over the months and years while sacrificing literally no quality and very, very minimal time and effort.

Eating Seasonally

Many fruits and vegetables are seasonal and are priced that way. Take advantage of it. On the west coast, where I live, fruits like cantaloupe, peaches, and strawberries are priced much lower in the summer. They also tend to taste much better during this time period when they are in season. In the winter, oranges and tangelos are priced much lower than at any other time of the year so it's a good time to eat more oranges versus other fruits that are not in season. If you enjoy and are able to eat a variety of different fruits and vegetables, try buying what is in season. It not only will taste better but it will also be much less expensive.

It's not hard to find out what fruits and vegetables are in season, and the prices will usually give you a good idea. Oftentimes, you will be able to find fruit and vegetables more than 50 percent off regular prices during peak season because they're plentiful. The chart below provides a quick example of some foods traditionally on sale during the summer and winter months and the difference in prices. Prices, of course, will vary depending on where you live, and these are averages taken from Southern California in select seasons.

	Price in Winter	Price in Summer	Approximate Price Difference	Optimal Time to Buy
Oranges	$0.40–$1.00/lb.	$0.89–$1.50/lb.	$0.50/lb	Winter
Cantaloupe	$2.00–$3.50 each	$0.50–$1.50 each	$1.50 each	Summer
Peaches	$1.25–$1.75/lb.	$0.75–$1.25/lb.	$0.50/lb	Summer
Strawberries	$2.00–$3.00/lb.	$1.00–$1.50/lb.	$1.00/lb	Summer
Broccoli	$0.79–$1.80/lb.	$1.30–$2.50/lb.	$0.50/lb	Winter
Zucchini	$2.00–$3.50/lb.	$1.00–$2.25/lb.	$1.00/lb	Summer

Based on the prices above, buying more peaches or cantaloupe versus oranges in the summer will save you money. Conversely, you would want to buy more oranges versus peaches or cantaloupe in the winter. The same goes for broccoli versus zucchini; purchase more broccoli in the winter, more zucchini in the summer. If you like various types of fruits and vegetables just the same, it would make sense to buy in season and on sale. Not only will you save but you will also notice a marked difference in freshness and taste.

Shopping at Produce Stores and Farmers' Markets

For fresh produce, try shopping at farmers' markets or produce stores instead of traditional grocery stores. Often, you will find much fresher food at lower costs than at the traditional grocery store. The grocery store is designed for convenience and is a place where you can get multiple items in one location. You are paying the price for this convenience. Remember this when purchasing any item at the grocery store. Ask yourself, can I get this somewhere else for a better price?

When deciding whether to shop for produce at the grocery store or a produce store, make sure to weigh the cost of time and fuel against any savings. In many cities, a produce store will be less than a half mile away from the grocery store, so it's very easy to make a trip to the grocery store first, then the produce store. At most, it's five to 10 minutes out of your way, probably less. However, if you live in a more rural area where the produce store is 30 to 40 minutes away, it may not be worth your while to go out of the way. Weigh savings against your time and fuel costs. These tips are designed to save you a little bit of money and give you a better product. If it becomes too complicated, it is not a strategy for you. It is never a good idea to make your personal finances too complicated. Simple is sustainable: the simpler the better.

Precut Fruits and Vegetables, Prepackaged Meals

Avoid precut fruits and vegetables as much as possible. They are marked up significantly higher and inherently can't be as fresh because they are literally already cut up. Often, you will pay more than two to three times as much for the convenience of precut fruit and vegetables, where it really doesn't save you much time. For example, a precut package of watermelon would probably only take the average person less than three to four minutes to cut up and package themselves. That's probably not worth spending two to three times the amount for the minimal convenience. An exception would be if you're "on the go" and maybe forgot your snack or lunch at home. Or maybe you're on a day trip and value the convenience. Precut fruits and vegetables are certainly a much healthier alternative than fast food or candy bars.

Another food item to avoid as much as possible are prepackaged small meals like lunch snack packs. Much like precut fruit and vegetables, pre-packaged lunches are significantly marked up. Of course, we all get busy during the year. You may have days or weeks that are exceptionally busy at work or in your personal life where you want to grab a quick, ready-made pack on the go. That's fine, you will have times like those. Just try to min-imize them and plan ahead as much as possible. Weigh your time against convenience and price to develop a plan best for you and your family. Plan ahead as much as possible so you're not in the position of having to make unwise financial decisions.

Coupons, Apps, and Other Saving Methods

Many people enjoy "bargain shopping," which can include cutting cou-pons, searching for online coupons, using cost savings apps, and other methods. These are not areas I personally use much but many people do with great success. When deciding to use one of these strategies, make sure that it is giving you a good return on your time spent. For example, if it takes you an hour per week to save $10 at the store, you are working for $10 an hour. If it's not an activity you enjoy, you may not want to work for that amount. On the other hand, if it takes you 15 minutes a week to save $30, that comes out to $120 an hour. That is a much greater return on your time so it will probably be worth it to you. Or if you really enjoy cutting coupons and searching the online apps, take advantage of the savings, even if they are minimal.

Keep It Simple

Saving money at the store is great. Saving money at the store with very minimal effort, or no effort, is even better. The tips contained in this chapter are designed to be simple and easy so that the actions become repeatable. When something like going to the grocery store becomes too complicated, people put a stop to the complicated activity and revert back to the old way of doing things. That is why I personally only implement basic strategies at the store and do not get into more time-consuming measures. If I can save $10–$15 a week on groceries by sticking to the basic principles found in this chapter, I consider it a success. If you multiply $15 a week by 52 weeks, that comes out to $780 per year. Not bad for almost no effort.

Action Step

Write down one item at the grocery store you can consistently get for a lower price.

CHAPTER 13

Tracking Your Money

Saving is a great habit, but without investing and tracking, it just sleeps.
— Manoj Arora

An important component to reaching your financial goals is tracking your money. This looks different for every person. Some people keep a notepad with them and handwrite everything they spend onto the notepad. Others enter their spending into their phone. Others use apps like Mint to automatically track spending and create reports.

Ultimately, the most important thing is to pick something that works for you and stick with it. You will be shocked and amazed at some of the things you are spending money on that add very little value to your life. You will be able to immediately eliminate items like this. Tracking is also a form of accountability. Research shows that when you write things down, you are more likely to hold yourself accountable and improve the target behavior. Best-selling author and expert on organizational leadership and employee engagement, Mark Murphy, notes, "Writing improves the encoding process."[19] This also works in other areas like diet and exercise but that's for another time.

I recommend tracking on a daily basis when you first start because you are learning a new skill. A new skill requires repetition and practice. Daily tracking provides you with the ability to build the money tracking skill and necessary repetition. As mentioned above, it really doesn't matter if you are using Mint, a notebook, or your phone. What matters is that you are track-ing consistently. There are literally hundreds of different systems out there, so I will simplify it into an easy to follow process involving minimal steps. The tracking tool below is easy and quick to use. The table below that is an example of how to track your spending.

Item	Date Purchased	Cost	Necessity?	If not a necessity, value number (1-10)

Item	Date Purchased	Cost	Necessity?	If not a necessity, value number (1-10)
Vacuum cleaner	1/10/19	$175	Yes	
Stainless Steel Trash can	1/10/19	$55	No	4
Jeans	1/12/19	$32	No	8
Softball shirt	1/17/19	$17	No	7
Video game	1/22/19	$30	No	6
Running shoes	1/29/19	$80	No	9
Dress shirt	1/30/19	$40	No	3
Dog food	1/30/19	$30	Yes	

The chart has you not only write down every purchase but also define whether it's a necessity, which will help you train your mind to really think about whether the item is a necessity or not. The chart then asks you to write down your value number, which will train your mind to only purchase things high on the value range. The goal is to only purchase necessities and highly valued items.

The next question is how detailed you want to get. It is easy to break down big items like vacuum cleaners and electronics, but what about the grocery store? Do you really need to itemize everything at the grocery store? That's a layered answer with some gray area. For best results, yes, itemize everything you purchase at the grocery store. Especially in the beginning. However, if that's not a sustainable plan, tracking groceries may not be for you. The key is to commit to a system that will be sustainable. The chart below is a template for tracking groceries or other small items.

Grocery Tracker

Grocery Item	Date Purchased	Cost	Reasonably Healthy and Necessary?	If not healthy and necessary, value number (1-10)

Grocery Tracker Example

Grocery Item	Date Purchased	Cost	Reasonably Healthy and Necessary?	If not healthy and necessary, value number (1-10)
9 Apples	4/1/19	$5.50	Yes	
15 oranges	4/1/19	$8.25	Yes	
Cheerios	4/1/19	$3.50	Yes	
Protein bars	4/1/19	$4.00	Yes	
Candy bar	4/1/19	$1.25	No	4
Pasta	4/1/19	$2.00	No	10
Carrots	4/1/19	$1.99	Yes	
Two bottles of wine	4/1/19	$11	No	9
Bananas	4/1/19	$3.00	Yes	
Chicken	4/1/19	$9.25	Yes	
Steak	4/1/19	$14	No	8
Salad	4/1/19	$3.50	Yes	
Candy	4/1/19	$1.50	No	2
Ravioli	4/1/19	$6.00	No	7
Salmon	4/1/19	$8.00	Yes	
Rice	4/1/19	$2.99	Yes	

Killing Two Birds with One Stone

Even though this is a book about personal finance, you can go a little further and add a note about whether or not the item is reasonably healthy. This is a way to kill two birds with one stone and keep yourself accountable regarding your personal finances and health with very little extra effort. In the example above, the person doing the shopping purchased mostly healthy items. Nutritionists could have a field day debating how healthy each item is, however, since this is a personal finance book, let's avoid the debate and list the category as "reasonably healthy."

In the example above, the person buying the groceries identified most items as reasonably healthy and necessary. We all need food to eat so there is no getting around this one. Most of the items they marked as not reasonably healthy or necessary earned high value ratings. Wine was rated very highly, as was steak. Maybe this person wants to make a nice dinner and have a couple glasses of wine. They value this food experience and are being intentional about it—there's nothing wrong with enjoying great food and wine. Notice that there are a few items rated as unhealthy, unnecessary, and with a low rating. Those are the items this person should strive to eliminate. In this example, it was candy and a candy bar. Those were probably impulse buys. Anyone who has ever been to a grocery store knows the candy and candy bars are placed in the checkout aisles to grab shoppers at the last minute.

Stop and Think

Impulse buys like candy bars, candy, and tabloid magazines are a great transition to the next principle: Stop and think before purchasing. This goes for both small and big items but especially big-ticket items. Anytime you are wanting to make an impulse buy, designate a period of time to wait. Wait at least 24 hours, preferably longer. This goes for online and retail stores too. If you have a sudden urge to purchase something online that's not a necessity, pause for the predetermined amount of time. If the purchase still feels right after the set amount of time, go ahead and make the purchase. The same goes for a retail store. This will require leaving the store and coming back to make the purchase. If you are willing to make the effort to come back to the store, the item probably holds a high value for you.

The stop and think principle is especially applicable for big purchases like cars, motorcycles, boats, jet skis, and other motorized devices. Avoid impulse buys on big ticket items at all costs. For the really big purchases, extend your cooling off period to at least one week. As good as it feels to drive off the lot with a brand-new car, it will feel equally as bad six months later when you realize the purchase was unwise and is going to set you back financially. Other large purchases include electronics like TVs, computers, tablets, and phones. In a perfect world, big ticket items will be preplanned, researched, and given an appropriate cooling off period before purchasing. Go back to your investor mindset: You are an investor who puts your money in income producing assets. Spending unwisely on large and small items is incongruent with the investor mindset.

Write it Down

Track your money and follow the systems put in place to help you succeed. These two steps alone will go a long way in building financial stability and eventually financial freedom. The very act of physically writing down what you are spending has an incredibly powerful effect on behavior. Writing it down makes you stop and think and really assess your values. It's building muscle memory and habit into your spending habits. Track your spending and you'll be amazed at the positive results and your mindset shift.

In addition to tracking your spending, it is important to perform scheduled financial reviews of your net worth. In other words, track your net worth. It's important that you understand where you are in your financial position so that you can both revise and create new goals. A yearly financial review of your net worth should be plenty. Some people like to review monthly or twice a year but yearly should suffice. You will also assess your investments at this time and make any necessary adjustments to your financial plan. You may decide you can increase your monthly spending or you may decide that you need to invest even more money in order to move toward your goals.

You Don't Need to Track Indefinitely

It's not necessary to track your spending forever. Tracking your money is simply a tool to help you build better financial habits. Once you have identified unnecessary spending and bad financial habits, you may not need to use this tool anymore. For example, there are many people who spend $10–$15 every work day on coffee and breakfast. Many of these people honestly have no intention of spending that much and don't want to either. They probably would be shocked to learn how much they are really spending. When they track their money, they realize just how much they spend on breakfast. This realization allows them to break the habit and form new behaviors that are more aligned to their financial and life values.

A solid month or two of tracking probably is enough to identify unwanted spending habits and gain clarity on your overall financial picture. Similar to the coffee and breakfast example, if someone learns via a tracking system that they are spending more than $400 per month on dinner takeout, they have identified the issue and can proceed to correct it. This person may not need to track indefinitely if they have identified and corrected the issue. Although tracking may not continue to be absolutely necessary, many people find they like the accountability that tracking provides and elect to continue.

Action Step

Track your money for one month. Use the system earlier in the chapter, create your own, or use an app like Mint. Note: once you start, you'll probably want to continue doing this every month.

CHAPTER 14

Money as a Partner, and Saving to Invest

*Never depend on single income. Make investment to
create a second source.*
– Warren Buffett

Too many people think of money as the enemy, as something to be feared.
This often leads to a lack of accountability about financial decisions. People
feel like their financial situation is something they cannot control so they
give up on it. Think of money as your partner, with you as the CEO. You
tell money what to do and where to go. You control how it's spent, how it's
invested, and how it's made. It is your responsibility as CEO to be accountable for the money decisions, good or bad. Money does not have a mind
of its own; you choose what to do with it and where to put it. *You* are in
complete control of your personal finances.

Money will behave the way you tell it to. Money does not talk back or
argue about where you are investing it or how you are spending it. It does
not get upset if you spend it on one thing or another. In a way, money is
the perfect partner; it does everything you ask, goes to work extra hard for
you over time, and if you treat it right, will eventually do most of the heavy
lifting. You will quickly become empowered by this mindset because you
have the control and ability to shape your future.

On his weekly podcast, *The Brian Buffini Show*, Brian Buffini perfectly
describes using money as a partner.[20] To paraphrase, he describes getting
up in the morning to shave or brush your teeth in preparation for work.

At work, you will earn money. While you are earning money at work, your investments will also be going to work for you. Any real estate investments you hold will be working for you, any money you have in stocks will be going to work for you, and any other investments you have will be going to work for you. You will have many partners working for you if you put them to work. You don't have to go at it alone in your financial journey. Money is your partner and is there to work for you. You just need to tell it what to do and it will work for you day and night, weekends and holidays, rain or shine.

A Respectful Partnership

Your partnership with money should be a relationship of respect. Any good partnership requires the leader (you) to at least be competent in the subject. To be a good partner with money, you must educate yourself and put into practice what you have learned. Education does not need to be the traditional type where you get a lecture from a teacher, read through a boring textbook, and answer questions at the end. Education comes in many forms—financial books, articles, blogs, discussions with friends/mentors, podcasts, and many more. Watching and/or being mentored by other financially successful people also qualifies as education.

One of the great things about personal finance and your relationship with money is that you don't have to know everything. Warren Buffett has said repeatedly, "Never invest in a business you can't understand." The same principle applies to personal finance. Much like with investing, you do not need to understand every little detail or strategy about personal finances. A successful investor can be anywhere from good to expert level in business, stocks, or real estate but does not need to invest in all of it to be successful. In your personal finances, you do not need to be good in multiple facets, just a few. Start with the simple principles like avoiding consumer debt, being intentional with your money, and clearly defining your goals. As you gain expertise in these areas, learn about other relevant principles and strategies. Being selective in your strategies is part of being a good partner with money.

A respectful relationship with your personal finances involves seeking advice and education from wise people. The real estate guru on late night infomercials who promises immediate riches with a couple hours of work every week "using other people's money" is probably not a wise person you should be seeking money advice from. Or your neighbor who has an "inside tip" on the next big stock that's going to be "bigger than Amazon and Apple combined." Take the time to vet people and determine if they are really qualified to give you financial advice. What kind of success have they had? Are they really financially successful, or are they just someone who likes to give unsolicited advice? Beware of the next shiny object. Respect your relationship with money because wealth rarely comes quickly or easily.

Part of a respectful relationship with money is sticking to your values, which will help avoid slipping into greed. Frequently revisit your values; they will guide you in your personal finances. If you have clearly defined values that you consistently follow, you are much less likely to fall into greed. Remember, greed involves making money just to make money, oftentimes neglecting the important things in your life just for the sake of accumulating money. Always let your values drive your actions—they will take you down the right path.

Saving to Invest

A critical part of your partnership with money is to invest it wisely. Like so many others, I was brought up to believe that you saved your money to buy things and have a little left over for a rainy day. That wasn't really saving money, it was more like saving money to spend later. It wasn't until much later in life that I established an investment mindset. An investing mindset will propel you to new heights and means you save your money specifically to invest and grow your capital. George S. Clason writes in his book, *The Richest Man in Babylon*:

> Every gold piece is to work for you. Every copper it earns is its child that can also earn for you. If you would become wealthy, then what you save must earn, and its children must earn, that all may help to give you the abundance you crave…. Then learn to make your treasure work for you. Make its children and its children's children work for you.[21]

As Clason writes, every gold piece is to work for you. You are now an investor. Investors don't just save, they save with the purpose to invest and grow their money. As your investments grow, new money will grow. The new money will also be invested and grow into new investments. Those investments grow and become new investments. It becomes an endless cycle of prosperity. This is how long-term wealth is created.

Compound Interest

The difference between earning interest and paying it is the difference between being wealthy and struggling financially. Money is a cycle. It will either cycle positively or negatively for you. It is your responsibility to educate
yourself and take control of your money cycle to ensure it cycles positively.

For example, suppose you start at $0. You go to work for the month
and save $200. Your neighbor also starts at $0, but instead of saving $200,
he spends $200 above what he earns. At the end of just one month, you
have $200 to invest and earn interest on. Your neighbor is $200 in the red
and now *owes* his creditors $200 plus interest. This is after just one month.
Take that month and compound it over time. Month after month you are
saving $200 per month and investing it. As the months and years pass, the
money you invest grows larger and larger, eventually making you wealthy.
Meanwhile, your neighbor is still living above his means by $200 per
month. However, the true cost is much greater than $200 every month.
Compounded over time, month after month, year after year, that $200 per
month turns into massive debt. Massive and hopeless to get out of.

You understand compound interest and your neighbor either does not
or chooses to ignore it. The chart below dives even deeper into the head to
head comparison.

	You	Your Neighbor	Difference
One Month	$200	-$200	$400
One Year	$2,640	-$2,561	$5,201
Five Years	$16,117	-$17,241	$33,358
Ten Years	$42,075	-$51,818	$93,893
Twenty Years	$151,206	-$260,249	$411,455

Assuming a 10 percent investment rate, $200 per month, and 14 percent interest rate on credit
card, spending rate of $200/month.

Note: Example provided shows no payments made on the debt to give a true side by side
comparison. In reality, creditors will require minimum payments and not allow you to borrow
this much money.

The numbers in the chart are astounding. He who understands compound interest has $151,206 invested after 20 years. He who does not

understand compound interest has $260,249 in debt. That is a staggering difference of $411,455 over a 20-year period!

An Unstoppable Force

Using time as your ally, compound interest becomes an almost unstoppable force. Consider the example of the flywheel that Jim Collins uses in his book, *Good to Great*.[22] The flywheel—a huge heavy, metal wheel mounted on an axle—takes great effort to move at first. It requires great effort to even inch it forward. You push, and push, and push, and the flywheel begins to move a little more. A quarter turn, a full turn, two turns. You continue to push hard and the flywheel really begins to move. Five turns, 10 turns, 100 turns. As the flywheel gathers momentum, you barely need to push at all to keep it going. The flywheel has gathered incredible momentum and is basically running on its own.

Investing and compound interest follow the same principle. It takes effort to begin investing. It is slow in the beginning—using the example above, you only have $200 after one month. That's not a life-changing amount. After two months you have a little more, and after a year you begin to notice. After five years, you really see it. After 20 years, your money has compounded to over $150,000. The flywheel is spinning and you barely push at all. Your money has gathered great momentum in the form of compound interest. You are on your way to financial freedom.

Invest 10 Percent or More

To maximize wealth potential, aim to invest at least 10 percent of your income. Don't just save 10 percent, invest 10 percent or more. As time passes, you will be able to invest more than 10 percent of your money and grow your wealth even quicker. I highly encourage you to exceed 10 percent as quickly as possible to really amplify your investment potential. Just as importantly, invest the money that your money earns. This is where the true power of compound interest occurs.

Look again at the example above in which $200 is invested monthly. Imagine the $200 moves up over the years to $300, $500, and eventually $1,000+. Now we are really utilizing compound interest and seeing life changing money.

---

22   Jim Collins, *Good to Great and the Social Sectors*, (New York: Harper, 2005).

Action Step

Set it up so that you automatically contribute 10 percent or more of your income every month to an investment account.

CHAPTER 15

Kids and Money

*If you want your children to turn out well, spend twice as much time with
them, and half as much money.*
– Abigail Van Buren

*We teach children to save their money. As an attempt to counteract
thoughtless and selfish expenditure, that has value. But it is not positive;
it does not lead the child into the safe and useful avenues of self-expression
or self-expenditure. To teach a child to invest and use is better
than to teach him to save.*
– Henry Ford

The previous chapter addressed how you should avoid comparing yourself
to others and the dangers of trying to keep up with the Joneses. Those of
you with kids know how easy it is to fall into the comparison trap on trivial
matters relating to your children. We compare how our kids dress, what
kind of toys they have, what kind of backpack they have, among other
things. But we don't have to do that. In the end, it's a futile, unproductive,
and massive waste of time.

The $200 Backpack
What if your friend's kid, Johnny, has a $200 backpack? So what! It doesn't

matter if Johnny has a $200 backpack or a free backpack his parents found on the street. It is a waste of time to compare trivial items like this. Instead, focus on important things like how your kids treat others, how they are progressing in school, and their nutrition. Focus on the important stuff; the trivial items are always forgettable anyway.

The Messy Kid House

We've all been to that house: The messy kid house. Toys everywhere: Princess castles, G.I. Joes, toy cars, marbles, balls, doll houses, forts, puzzles, trading cards, games. You name it, it's on the living room floor. You can barely tell if the flooring is carpet or hardwood because it's covered with so many toys. Why all the toys? What is the purpose? Is having all these toys really improving children's lives? What about the parents? Is their life better with toys sprawled throughout the house?

As parents, we want the best for our children. For many, that has somehow translated into buying them "stuff." And stuff, and stuff, and more stuff. We may not even realize we're doing it. Suddenly, we can't see the floor anymore because it's completely covered with toys. We buy a toy and we feel good because we're trying to give our kids the best. The cumulative effect of buying all these toys is not only on the floor space though.

The cost of all these toys and "stuff" is high. Spend $14.99 here, $25 there, $3.99 here, $29.99 for something a little bigger. The cost of toys adds up. Over the weeks, months, and years, the costs are significant. Many parents spend thousands on toys every year only to see them looked at once and thrown on the floor. It's wasteful and costly—two negatives. It's also a bad lesson for our kids. The lesson becomes: Look at something once, then move on to the next shiny object. Next, next, next.

The Shiny Object Syndrome

Does the shiny object syndrome sound familiar? Is it possible that kids raised to always move on to the next shiny object maintain that habit as they enter adulthood? Look at the way car companies market to adults as just one example among many:
- You deserve the best.
- It's Christmas time, you deserve a new luxury car as a gift. And it will be parked in the driveway of your luxury house with a nice bow.

- Dads are much cooler if they have the newest, fastest, yet family friendly, sedan.
- Everyone deserves a new car.
- Your neighbors will envy you.
- Low monthly payments.
- Cash back.
- Driving is life.
- Lease it, the payments are affordable.
- Summertime: beach, fun, brand new car.
- Trade in that old car today, you deserve better than that.

Car companies have appealed to the next shiny object syndrome for years. They spend millions in advertising appealing specifically to our desire for the next best thing. See any familiarities with the way toys are marketed?

Look Familiar?

Toy Companies	Car Companies
Gotta have the newest and best.	Buy the newest and best car.
This toy really is the best.	No other car comes close to this one.
Hot new thing, all the kids are getting it.	This car has everything, all your friends will envy you and want one.
Kids gathered around all playing the new game.	Fun, sun, bonfires at the beach, friends.
Fun with friends.	Driving around friends, everyone laughing.

Is there a correlation that parents who buy their kids the newest and fanciest toys are the best parents and have the most well-behaved, smartest kids? I have yet to see that study. The truth is, you are not a bad parent if you don't buy your children massive amounts of toys.

By no means am I suggesting you never buy your child a toy. I have two kids of my own and buy them toys. I think kids *should* have toys. They're fun, encourage kids to use their imagination, and give them something to do as a group, among many other benefits. What I am saying is that it is OK to limit the number of toys. Toys do not need to be sprawled all over the house for kids to enjoy them. Toys don't need to number in the hundreds for kids to enjoy them either.

Don't feel guilty if you aren't buying your kids each and every toy they see or want. That does not make you a bad parent. Think about your values again. What do you want to teach your children? How do you want to raise them, what do you want them to value? Do you want them to value "stuff?" And hey, when it's all said and done, your kid is probably going to play more with the box than the actual toy anyway.

Teaching Your Kids About Money

Most schools do not provide education about personal finance. That's not to say that schools aren't great; they provide tremendous value both socially and educationally. They just don't teach your kids about personal finance. The credit card companies know this, which is why young adults receive endless credit card offers. It's also why credit card companies used to swarm college campuses with "free stuff" just for applying for a card. That was prior to the 2009 Credit Card Accountability, Responsibility, and Disclosure (CARD) Act that significantly limited this practice.[23] The credit card companies know that young adults have little to no financial education so they market to them heavily to acquire lifelong customers.

If schools don't provide financial education, then it's up to you as a parent to do that. That begs the question, how? The "how" goes back to your individual and family values as it pertains to personal finances. What do you want your kids to learn? What values do you want to instill? The answers to those questions will drive how you teach them about personal finance. You don't need a formal curriculum, but it will help you to develop a few principles and strategies. Teaching will also evolve over the years as your child gets older and more mature. It goes without saying that you won't teach your five-year-old the same as you would a senior in high school.

Your Children Are Watching

To teach your children about personal finance, start by being a good example. Like anything in life, your kids are watching your every move, and the same goes with how you handle your personal finances. If you spend every penny you have, your kids will think it's normal to spend every penny they have. If you save and invest over 10 percent of your income, your kids will think it's normal to save and invest at least 10 percent of the money they get from birthdays and allowance. If you sit down with your spouse and talk calmly about money, your kids will pick up that money conversations are conducted in a calm and organized manner. On the other hand, if you and your spouse constantly fight and bicker about money, your kids will learn that money is something to be feared and fought about.

Going back to your values, what do you want to teach your kids about personal finance? There are infinite ways to provide money lessons; the most important part is identifying what you want to teach. Three main areas that many people focus on are:

1. Your value system
2. Possible lessons to be taught
3. Principle to be applied

The table below outlines a few examples of how you can organize what you teach your kids. The table immediately following is for you to use as a resource.

Financial Value (From Your Value System)	Possible Lessons	Principle
Spending focused on necessities and what you highly value.	- Make a list with your child before going to the grocery store. - Identify clothes to be bought before going online or to the store.	Be intentional with shopping, utilize tools like lists.
Saving and investing part of the money you make.	- Set aside at least 10 percent of your child's allowance with them, go to the bank (physical branch or online) together and deposit the money. Match their contributions up to a certain dollar amount. - Teach children about compound interest and how investing a small part of their money makes a big difference.	Save and invest 10 percent or more of your income and 10 percent of your child's money, invest it wisely.

| Knowing how much money you have. | - Involve your kids when you track your income.
- Teach your kids to track their income, set up tools for them. | Track your spending. |

Financial Value (From Your Value System)	Possible Lessons	Principle

There are endless ways to teach your children about money, these are just a few very brief examples. What are your values? How can you translate those values into teachable moments? What principles can you share with your children? Remember, your kids are watching and paying attention. Start with leading by example, then provide them with financial lessons aligning with your personal and family values.

Mindset: You CAN Save and Invest with Kids

We've all heard the reasons you can't save and invest money with kids. You may have even used some of these reasons yourself, such as:

- "Now that we have kids, we can't save any money."
- "All of our money goes to our kids; we can't get ahead."
- "Daycare is so expensive; we can't possibly save."
- "With clothes and food to pay for, we don't save like we used to."
- "Investing? That's for rich people or people who have no kids."
- "Investing with kids? Get real."

Think back to the principle from Clason's book, *The Richest Man in Babylon*. Part of what you earn is yours to keep. There are no parentheses after that statement indicating, "unless you have kids." The book recommends investing at least 10 percent of your income. That principle does not change just because you have children. Find ways to adjust your money to align with this principle. Focus heavily on paying yourself first and you will be able to continue saving and investing.

Financial Advantages to Having Children

Wait, are you saying that there are financial benefits to having children? Yes! One of the obvious advantages is the tax benefits in the form of deductions. Talk with your CPA or tax professional about what those are, as they are different in every state. Make sure to take advantage of these deductions. Childcare tax deductions in addition to others can be significant.

A not-so-obvious financial advantage to having children is the elimination of some of the costs you used to incur. More than likely when you have kids, you won't go out as much as you used to. That's not to say the fun is gone in your life, your time is just adjusted to spend more time with your family and children, and you participate in different types of activities. Think of it as reallocating your money and time when you have kids; it's a reorganization of your priorities. Your expenses will go up for things like diapers, childcare, and clothes, but they will also go down for things like going out for drinks and spur of the moment weekend trips. Embrace the life change and focus on effectively adjusting your priorities and personal finances.

You can save and invest your money with kids. Just like any life adjustment, it requires an assessment of your values and working towards new goals. The answers may not always be easy or obvious but they are out there. Next, I'll touch on some additional ways to save money with kids.

Childcare

For households with two working parents, one of the biggest expenses is childcare, especially during the infant stage. According to the Economic Policy Institute, yearly infant care in the United States ranges from $5,436 (Mississippi) all the way up to $24,243 (Washington, DC).[24] This is incredibly expensive. A great way to save money in the child's first few months of life is to carefully look at your benefits at work. Find out how much time you can take off between you and your spouse while getting either full or partial pay. That extra time not only helps reduce childcare costs but improves parent/child bonding time.

After both parents have exhausted their time off from work while getting paid full or half wage, think about relatives and friends who can watch the baby. Grandparents love spending time with their grandkids and will probably be more than willing to help out with childcare. Other relatives such as aunts, uncles, and cousins may also be willing to help out. Schedule relatives by the week or day, whatever works best for your family situation. You will be surprised about how willing people are to help.

Trusted friends are another great option for childcare, especially friends with small children themselves. Many people do a childcare pool where one friend takes set days and the other friend fills in the other days. This kind of arrangement works especially well for parents with a somewhat-flexible work schedule. Childcare pools can also consist of one family picking up all the kids on certain days of the week and another family picking up the other days. This kind of arrangement minimizes, and can even eliminate, the need for after school care. These are only a couple ways to utilize the help of friends. Think about the friends you have and how you can all help each other.

Here's an example: James Lewis picks up his two kids from school along with the two Smith kids every Monday, Wednesday, and Friday. The kids hang out at the Lewis house those days until the Smiths arrive home at 5:30 p.m. On Tuesdays and Thursdays, Tanya Smith picks up her two kids along with the two Lewis kids and everyone hangs out at her house until 6:00 p.m. when the Lewis's arrive home.

Childcare does not have to be an all or nothing situation. You may be able to mix and match traditional childcare with friends and relatives. For example, your child goes to daycare three days a week and to their grandparents the other two days. That type of arrangement will likely reduce the childcare costs paid to daycare or preschool. Some preschools and daycare centers also have half-day options, which may also reduce your out-of-pocket costs. Be creative, explore all options and create favorable circumstances for you and your family.

Clothes

Clothes are another huge expense when you have kids. Fortunately, there are ways to save money in this area as well. Hand-me-downs are a great clothing option, especially when kids are young and don't care what they're wearing. Kids grow so quickly—it makes a lot of sense to use hand-me-downs so that you're not buying new clothes every couple months. Friends, relatives, and older siblings are great sources for secondhand clothes. It's easy to establish networks with friends and relatives where you pass on clothes from child to child. When your child outgrows the clothes, pass them on to a friend or family member to continue the cycle.

As children get older, they may not want to wear hand-me-downs. That's OK. Go back to your value system and what you have taught your children. Your children probably will not value buying the most expensive and newest pair of shoes. They likely will be just fine buying medium-priced clothing and shoes. Just like with anything else, it doesn't have to be an all-or-nothing proposition. Your children can always mix and match more expensive brand name clothes with lesser-priced items. For example, your almost full grown teenage son may have an expensive, high-quality jacket that is likely to last for multiple years while wearing an inexpensive pair of jeans because he tends to wear them out quicker. Or he might have an expensive pair of shoes for basketball, while his everyday shoes are low to medium cost. Teenagers can also get a part-time job or use their allowance if they want more expensive clothes.

Allowance and Part-Time Jobs

As your children move to the early elementary years, they probably will become interested in finding small ways to make money to buy toys or games on their own or with some help from you. Allowance is a great way for kids to earn money on their own. For many parents, the buck stops there: their child works for allowance, parent gives them the money, and they spend it or put some in their drawer or piggy bank.

However, that doesn't have to be the end of it. The distribution of allowance is a fantastic time to teach your children about money. Rather than just handing over the money, take the time to sit down with your children and talk about what they are going to do with it. Ask them what they really want with the money; their answers might surprise you. These are the beginning steps to the establishment of their own values.

Talk with them about investing 10 percent or more (ideally 20–30 percent) of the money and then work with them to automate it. Set up an online account that automatically takes at least 10 percent of their allowance to invest. Give them access to the account so they can see their money grow. Sit down with them and do it together as a family. You can even try matching them dollar for dollar up to a certain amount.

As your children grow older, their skills and knowledge will evolve. Adjust the financial lessons as you see fit. Maybe your child will want to invest more than 10 percent of their money, or maybe they will ask you why it's important to save. Keep educating and supporting them through the process. Eventually, the allowance will probably transition into a part-time job. The principle remains the same: They should save and invest at least 10 percent of the money they earn. Be creative and set up a "match program" where you match a portion of their contributions. Give them books to read like George S. Clason's *The Richest Man in Babylon*, David Bach's *The Latte Factor*, and Robert Kiyosaki's *Rich Dad, Poor Dad*. Remember, most schools don't teach kids about money, so this is your opportunity as a parent to mold your children and set them up for a lifetime of financial success.

Paying for College

Student loan debt can be crippling and is out of control for many families. Many parents of young children would like to save for their own children's college but many are still paying off massive amounts of student loan debt themselves. Student loans have become an ugly, generational cycle of debt. According to *Forbes*, total student loan debt is over $1.5 trillion in the United States alone! About 44.7 million people have student loan debt, with the average amount of debt being $28,650.[25]

Explore Alternative Strategies to Pay for College

Paying for college is incredibly expensive and a huge challenge. Are there any available options other than having your son or daughter being saddled with massive student loan debt or going into debt yourself to pay for their college? The traditional way most people save for college is putting money into a tax advantaged 529 plan or savings account. There is nothing wrong with saving this way; it will eventually get the job done provided enough money is saved. However, this is not the only way to pay for college, and to be honest, not everyone can afford to save in this way. With college costs at an all-time high and with parents saddled with student debt themselves, it's important to look at all viable options. Think outside the box, and don't leave any stones unturned.

There are literally hundreds of websites and blogs that are dedicated to helping parents and students find strategies to pay for college. Go through at least a few of them to get ideas; it will be well worth your time. For example, say you spend 30 hours looking at websites and taking suggested actions. If you can save $5,000 in tuition, that's $167 per hour tax free! Unless your job or investments pay more than that, I'd say that's a great use of your time. To conclude, here are a few alternative strategies to get you started, along with a few websites worth exploring. Be careful of some of the websites because they contain advertisements, but there is some good info shared on each site.

Strategies:
- Scholarships: athletic, academic, private
- Junior college for general requirements
- AP classes in high school that qualify for college credit
- Grants

- Work study programs
- Invest in real estate instead of a savings plan—cash out refinance or use monthly rent to pay for college
- Purchase real estate near campus for your child to live in and rent out to friends
- Live off campus
- GI Bill
- Apply for as much financial aid as possible
- Look at public universities in-state
- Ask friends and family for creative ideas
- Search online using different keywords

Websites:

- https://www.usnews.com/education/blogs/the-college-solution/2010/06/15/the-10-best-college-websites
- https://studentloanhero.com/featured/college-search-engine-find-dream-school/
- https://www.simpletuition.com/managing-finances/alternative-ways-to-pay-for-college/
- https://studentloanhero.com/featured/how-to-pay-for-college-strategies-help-you/
- https://clark.com/education/9-ways-to-pay-for-college-without-student-loans/
- https://www.collegevaluesonline.com/features/unique-ways-to-pay-for-college-that-dont-involve-loans/

Kids and Money Summarized: Find Out What Works for Your Family

Raising kids is expensive—there's no doubt about it. That said, there are ways to make raising kids less expensive. You just have to find the ways that work for you and your family. What works for one family may not work for another. One family may be fine using hand-me-downs, while that doesn't work for another family. One family may have lots of relatives and friends that can help out with childcare, while other families may be new to an area and not have that option. Every family is going to have their advantages and challenges. It's about making it work for your particular situation and values. Work with your children to learn about money and find the teachable moments. As they grow older, work with them to fund their advanced education using creative strategies.

Action Steps

1. What are the top three things you value with your kids? For example, spending time together, education, or sports. Focus your financial efforts in these areas.

2. What is one area you are spending money on that you and your children don't value. For example, extra toys, music lessons your child hates, or takeout food. Eliminate that item and put the money toward something you value instead.

CHAPTER 16

Your Most Important Money Partner: Your Significant Other

Money may not buy love, but fighting about it will bankrupt your relationship.
– Michelle Singletary

Your most important financial partner by far is your significant other. Your goals must be aligned. It may sound cliché but both people need to be pulling in the same direction. If you and your significant other are not aligned in your goals, that means you are pulling in opposite directions and will get way off track. Even worse, you will go nowhere while arguing and resenting each other. Set up a structure and routine so that the two of you are reviewing your finances and goals routinely. That may mean a weekly or monthly sit down or casual conversations throughout the month. The important thing is to be aligned.

Opposites Crash and Burn

There's an old saying that "opposites attract." This may be the case, but when it comes to money, opposites usually end up crashing and burning. Imagine a scenario in which Partner A wants early financial freedom and Partner B wants to spend the majority of his or her paycheck on "stuff." These two people are completely out of balance and are likely to end up fighting about money, resenting each other, and possibly ending up a divorce statistic. Partner A is going to see Partner B as getting in the way of his or her financial goals. Partner B is going to see Partner A as cheap and out of tune with his or her needs. Unless there's a drastic change in one person's values, the road ahead promises to be difficult. Even with some compromise from each person, they are going to be pretty far off in their life and financial values.

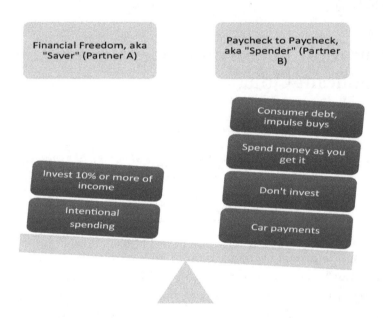

Partner A and Partner B are way off balance. The scale is leaning far to the right, which means these two people are not in financial harmony. Not only are they not in financial harmony but they are really far away from it. These are major financial obstacles that will be challenging to bring back in harmony.

The number one thing couples argue about is money.[26] Financial incompatibility is a major problem and needs to be addressed.

Somehow, society has made conversations about money taboo. People are embarrassed to talk about their personal finances and avoid it like

---

26   Sharon Feiereisen, "The 12 Biggest Money-Related Reasons People Get Divorced," *Business Insider*, (July 7, 2019), https://www.businessinsider.com/divorce-money-issues-financial-relationship-couple-2019-7.

the plague. Unfortunately, this has trickled down to relationships where spouses and long-term partners feel like they can't have money conversations until one person finally has had enough and blows up at the other person for purchasing something they didn't agree with. This is extremely dangerous and unfortunate. The good news is that it's all preventable by proactively having money conversations well before any one person gets frustrated. Ideally, those conversations will take place *before* getting into a serious relationship but that's not often the case. Whether those conversations happened pre-serious relationship or not, it's imperative that each partner communicate their needs, goals, and wants. Work together to establish common financial goals and listen to one another.

Today is the next best day to start. Align your goals, get on the same page, and proceed with your plan. The principles outlined in this book are a great starting point for this kind of conversation. Hiring a financial coach who can act as an objective third party and cool-headed facilitator may also help.

Before Picking a Partner

In a perfect world, money conversations would occur well before a long-term commitment is made to another person. If you are reading this book pre-marriage or serious relationship, this section is for you. If you are already married or in a serious relationship, you can skip to the next section on working as a team.

Hopefully, as you are becoming more serious with someone, you will get an idea of how they feel about money. Look for the clues. If he or she has a low paying job with no other income source, drives a luxury car, has consumer debt, and is always complaining about having no money, you probably can assume he or she is irresponsible with money. If, on the other hand, he or she has an average to above average paying job and talks about how important it is to have control of his or her finances, you can probably assume this person is responsible with money. The signs and clues will be there, you just have to look for them. It's easy to be smitten and ignore the signs or make excuses. As difficult as it may be, watch for the signs and save yourself the trouble over the long haul.

So now you've looked for the clues and things seem compatible financially and in other ways. You decide that this person may be right for you and you want to have the "money conversation." The best way to do this is to just do it. Your partner will probably be relieved that you brought it up first. Remember to be open and honest, respect their opinion, and follow Stephen Covey's principle of "seek first to understand, then to be understood." Make a concerted effort to understand each other and work together to find solutions.

What Is Your Partner's Money History?

Everyone comes into a relationship with baggage. Some come with a little baggage and others come with baggage that will make the average person want to run for the hills. What kind of money baggage does your partner come with? Do they have hundreds of thousands in student loan debt? Are they a spender despite being in massive debt? Is your partner carrying five maxed out credit cards in his or her wallet? Are your financial goals hopelessly far apart? Is your partner afraid to spend any money whatsoever in fear that they won't be able to earn more money? Was your partner brought up to feel guilty about money? Are you so far apart that you can't see this relationship working out?

As uncomfortable as learning the answers to these questions might be, it is critical that they be answered to your satisfaction. It is OK for you to value certain characteristics in a partner and to set healthy boundaries. If you have a partner who is far out of alignment with your values, that is a problem that needs to be addressed sooner than later. You have high standards and deserve to be with someone who meets those standards. It's not romantic or something you hear in fairytales but an important issue nevertheless.

Jim and Andrea: A Story of Financial Reckoning

Jim came from a middle-class family in the San Francisco Bay Area. His family was not rich but they were comfortable. Jim pretty much got whatever he wanted growing up. If he wanted a toy, he just had to ask his mom or dad and they would buy it for him. As he got into high school, Jim's parents bought him a car for his 16th birthday and paid for him to go to an expensive out of state college. Jim didn't work throughout college but was never short on cash because his mom and dad made sure he was well-funded. Jim never worried about money because it was always there when he needed it. His cell phone was always paid for and his tuition was billed straight to his parents. Jim didn't live a lavish lifestyle but money was never a problem for him. He wasn't spoiled but he never had to think or worry about money.

Andrea also grew up in a middle-class background. Like Jim, her family wasn't rich, but they weren't hurting for money either. From an early age, Andrea's parents made it a point to teach her about money. This meant little lessons throughout early childhood and a part-time job in high school and college. Andrea's parents were determined that their daughter was going to understand money. In high school, Andrea sometimes complained to her parents that all her friends got new cars and didn't have to work. She wondered why she had to work and save a percentage of her paycheck while her friends just got what they wanted. She was a kid after all, so why did she have to be so "adult" with money?

Although Jim and Andrea came from similar socioeconomic backgrounds, they thought very differently about personal finances. By the time she was 26, Andrea already owned her own condo which she had paid for in cash. She even took in a roommate at $600 a month in rent. Every month, she put all $600 that she received from her roommate into an index fund. She thought it was a great deal that her roommate was literally funding her eventual financial freedom. In addition to the $600 rent, she put every pay raise into an index fund. She calculated that by the time she was 30, she'd be contributing more than $2,500 per month into her investments just by combining rent money with her pay increases.

Meanwhile, Jim was living it up. He had almost no savings, a $475 car payment, and two large credit card bills. Things weren't as easy as they were when he was in high school and college. Although his mom and dad would still send him a check when he couldn't pay the minimum on his credit cards, Jim was struggling to get by. He thought he was doing fine and figured people in their twenties were supposed to struggle and have debt.

Andrea and Jim met through a mutual friend and instantly liked each other. After several dates, Andrea was starting to think this guy might be someone she'd like to date more seriously. Every time they went out, though, Jim would make little jokes or comments that the date was putting him in the poorhouse, even though Andrea paid for at least half of their outings. On one of the dates, Jim even had his credit card declined. He said it was a "misunderstanding," and asked Andrea if she could "spot him on this one." She didn't mind paying, but the warning bells were starting to go off.

The two went out on a few more dates and honestly had a good time with each other. However, something inside Andrea kept telling her that something wasn't quite right. Finally, on one of the dates, she commented to Jim that he seemed to be a little worried about money. Jim said it was cool and he just had to catch up a little bit. As they kept talking, Jim made the comment that credit cards were a "lifesaver," and he was waiting for his mom and dad to help him pay them off. Jim said that his parents always helped him out and they would be giving him a check for $7,500 once they found out he was struggling.

Jim and Andrea continued to go out, but Andrea wasn't really feeling it anymore. She liked Jim enough, but had a lot of doubts about his attitudes about money and other things. This wasn't the kind of guy she saw herself with long term. Things naturally just started to fizzle out and Andrea felt a sense of relief about the direction they were going. There were no hard feelings, but Andrea knew she and Jim were too far apart on their financial and life goals to have anything serious.

Work on Money as a Team

Think of this scenario: You and your significant other are on a game show and have 90 seconds to read a map, go through an obstacle course, and find the hidden treasure. If you find the hidden treasure together, you'll win $150,000! How will you and your spouse interact during this 90 second opportunity to win $150,000? Will you avoid conversations about the map and change the subject? Will you fight about it during those valuable 90 seconds? Will the map become a taboo subject? Or will you focus and cooperate together and work towards the goal?

Of course, you will cooperate and work together. Work on your finances as if you were on a game show with a chance to win the treasure. Focus on working as a team towards a common goal. This means establishing a mindset that you are in this together and will put the needs of the team first. Fighting, squabbling, and bickering have no place in anyone's financial journey. It wastes time and creates hostility and resentment toward each other.

You've probably heard many people say that money is one of the primary causes of relationship problems in the United States. Not true. *Fighting* about money is the problem. Create a mindset early in your relationship that money is a team sport and not something to be arguing about. Open and honest discussions, yes. Arguing and bickering, no.

It is easy to say that you shouldn't argue about money. It may even be easy to promise to your significant other that you won't fight about money. However, putting that into practice is a different story. People are human and have human emotions. We get frustrated and have our opinions and viewpoints. We all think we are right (and not just about money). People also have different backgrounds when it comes to money. So it's a challenge to combine those different experiences with our basic human emotions. We must recognize the challenges and develop ways to overcome them.

Just like anything else in a relationship, find out where your partner is coming from and what they value. Think back to Chapters 1 and 2, which discussed values. What does your partner value? What is most important to them? How can you help your partner migrate their personal goals to being team goals that a relationship requires? Really listen to the other side and come in with the mindset that you may not be right about everything. Once you understand what your partner values, open and honest conversations can take place. Work together to figure out what you value together and work towards those identified values.

Get It Out in the Open

Get all your feelings out in the open. So many people allow years of frustration over money to be pent-up and explode into anger. This can lead to a variety of relationship-damaging things such as passive aggressive behavior, outright aggressive behavior, and big fights about money. Money is a topic that needs to be talked about and worked on together. Years of silence and dissatisfaction does not come without consequences. Money is not the enemy; the enemy is fighting with your significant other about money. Being on the same financial page with your significant other will make things infinitely smoother. If you make the right choice in a partner and take the time to plan things out and talk about goals, your chances of financial success are much greater. Your day to day happiness will probably be greater too.

Action Step

If you are in a long-term relationship, think of one step you can personally take that will help you work more cooperatively with your significant other regarding money. If you are single, think of one step you can take to improve your financial situation.

CHAPTER 17

Goal Setting

Setting goals is the first step in turning the invisible into the visible.
– Tony Robbins

At this point of the book, we've hopefully established our values, changed our mindset on things like financing luxury items, and have stopped comparing ourselves to the Joneses. In this chapter, we are going to use all that knowledge to set goals. There is tremendous power in setting goals because it provides us with an actual plan or roadmap. Motivational speaker and self-development author Brian Tracy says, "A goal without a plan is only a dream." The Cheshire Cat in the children's book *Alice in Wonderland* tells us, "If you don't know where you want to go, it doesn't matter which path you take." Goals turn your dreams into plans and provide you with the roadmap so you know which path to take. Make the Cheshire Cat proud and begin to set goals!

Short-Term Goals

Everyone must start somewhere. We can't all go from zero to 1,000 in an hour. Short-term goals are that starting place. Short-term goals get you a quick win to build your confidence, taste success, and make progress toward longer-term goals. Short-term goals are critical because they are the first action step to build momentum. The accumulation of short-term goals adds up to medium- and long-term goals. Short-term goals force you to take immediate action and implement manageable action steps.

The chart below lists some sample short-term goals along with two very attainable action steps to help you move toward that goal. This is a great way to simplify goals and make them more achievable. Always ask yourself, what is the next action step I need to take? A series of seemingly small action steps lead to big results. For example, before I began writing the first draft of this book, I told myself I would write one page a day. After one week, I had seven pages. After two weeks, I had 14. It didn't seem like a lot. But after 10 weeks, I had more than 70 pages, which did seem like a lot and gave me the momentum and inspiration to keep going. Without those small action steps, I probably would have given up.

Short-Term Financial Goal	First Action Step	Second Action Step
Spend under $100 on this week's groceries.	Take 15 minutes to meal plan for the week.	Make a shopping list and include only items needed to make planned meals.
Bring your lunch to work four out of five days this week.	Take your lunch bag out of the closet and put it where you can see it.	Go to the store and purchase enough food for four lunches.
Make your own coffee three to five days this week.	Take the coffee pot out of the pantry and put on the counter.	Put three filters next to coffee pot.
Only use the vending machine at work once this week.	Take all the money out of your wallet except for $2 to be used for vending machine.	Pack a bag of nonperishable, healthy snacks to bring to work. Leave some in your desk.
Spend under $50 at the bar Friday night.	Take only $50 cash with you to the bar.	Enjoy dinner and drinks at home or a friend's house before going out.

What are some of your short-term financial goals? What actions steps do you need to take? You can use this template or create something on your own. It doesn't matter what you use, it just matters that you are writing them down.

Short Term Financial Goal	First Action Step	Second Action Step

Medium-Range Financial Goals

Now it's time to think bigger. Let's move on to medium range goals. For most people, medium-range goals would take place somewhere between six months to five years. There are no right or wrong answers; the important part is that you put thought and action into the process. Where do you foresee yourself financially in two years? What do you want to accomplish? How are you going to get there? The development and progression toward medium range goals are an instrumental step in reaching your long-term life goals. It is imperative that you make progress toward medium-range goals or you'll be running in quicksand; you'll be in the same spot year after year, feeling stuck, and asking yourself the same old questions. The chart below provides examples of medium-range goals, along with potential action steps.

Medium-Range Financial Goal	Action Step 1	Action Step 2
Save $24,000 in two years.	Get a side hustle, put all proceeds into account.	Get a roommate, put all money collected into account.
Pay off $12,000 car note in one year.	Increase your autopay from $450/month to $1,000/month.	Have garage sale, immediately put proceeds towards car note.
Invest 10 percent of your paycheck for the year.	Open your computer and create an online investment account.	Set up the online investment account to automatically deduct 10 percent of your paycheck.
Max out Roth IRA this year ($6,000).	Create Roth IRA account online.	Automate savings in Roth IRA account to $500/month.
Purchase a rental property in the next three years.	Read five books about real estate investing.	Identify two potential markets to invest in, call five agents in each marketplace.

What are your medium-range financial goals? What attainable action steps can you implement immediately to move toward your goals?

Medium-Range Financial Goal	First Action Step	Second Action Step

Long-Term Financial Goals

Long-term financial goals should be purposefully big, life changing goals. Long-term goals are well-thought-out and are a direct reflection of your value system. They are usually five years or more away but can be reached more quickly with careful and concise planning and consistent actions. Think big when you develop your long-term financial goals. What have you always wanted out of life? What do you feel like you can accomplish? How can reaching a specific long-term financial goal impact your life in other areas? For example, if a long-term goal of yours is to be financially independent (where you don't need to work anymore to cover living expenses) by age 50, how would that impact the rest of your life? How would it impact your spiritual and physical health? Your ability to travel? Your ability to spend more time with your kids?

Think very carefully about your long-term financial goals and how they impact and interact with your other life goals. As you develop your long-term goals, you will likely realize there is a synergy between them. That's a good thing. It's one clear indicator that your life is in sync, which includes your value systems, career, family goals, among other things.

Long-Term Financial Goal	Action Step 1	Action Step 2
Be financially independent by age 50.	Calculate how much money you'll need to be financially independent at that age.	Set up a monthly plan to reach that amount of money.
Send both kids to college without student loans.	Develop strategy to pay for college.	Research probable costs for college in the years your children will likely attend.
Have today's equivalent to $10,000 per month in passive income stream in 15 years.	Develop an investment strategy.	Calculate what you'll need to allocate over the next year to obtain that goal, then automate it.
Pay off home by age 50.	Ensure you already have best possible interest rate. If not, refinance into optimal rate.	Develop pay down strategy and make it automatic (there are many available).

What are your long-term financial goals? Take your time on this exercise— it should be a deep self-reflection and shouldn't be rushed. This may take several days, and expect to come back to it and make multiple revisions.

Long-Term Financial Goal	First Action Step	Second Action Step

Shared Goals

Personal finance goals are not written or developed in a vacuum. They intertwine with your family life, value system, and current position in life. Therefore, it's important to develop and share goals as a team, namely your partner or spouse. As your children get older, you may even want to work on goals as a family. That's also an opportunity to teach your children more in-depth about personal finance.

Shared goals create a blueprint for future financial expectations. If all parties are working toward the same goal, there is much less of a chance for future discord or straying from the plan. Basic human nature tells us that when people are involved and actively engaged with a plan, they are much more likely to follow that plan. Actively involve your partner and make it a true collaboration. End with both of you having the same expectations and understanding of the plan. This may take some time but be patient and really work as a team. With so many relationships negatively impacted by money, wouldn't it be great to have a plan in place to prevent conflict?

Written Goals

Write out your financial goals. There is something about "writing it down" that has a great effect on the mind. It's like giving your mind written instructions and leaving it out for your brain to see on a daily basis. Your brain can't help but follow the instructions. Written goals directly counter the adage, "Out of sight, out of mind."

Writing out your financial goals also requires you to think more about them than if you just talk about them. There is something very powerful about putting pen to paper or typing out your goals. There is a certain thought process that takes place, requiring you to think hard about your goals and how they align with your values. When people take the time to write things down, the final product is typically a much higher quality than when just talked about. Written goals are real and have a way of keeping people accountable.

Revising and Posting Goals

Setting goals, writing them down, and working with a partner are great. However, that's not enough. Goals must also be revisited and revised. Schedule time to review and revise your goals. Whoever helped write the goals should also be involved in the revision of the goals. For example, a single woman who developed goals on her own would only need to review the goals on her own. However, a married man who developed his goals with his wife and two high school aged children would want to involve those family members in the revision of goals.

In addition to scheduled times to review and revise goals, having goals posted where you will see them every day will exponentially increase your likelihood of success. Some people like to post them in their office, home office, bathroom, closet, or anywhere where they will see them every day and think about them. Remember the quote from Earl Nightingale: "The mind moves in the direction of our currently dominant thoughts." Posting goals in a prominent place where you can see them every day naturally prompts us to think about them and be accountable. That daily interaction with our goals is what leads to them becoming our "dominant thoughts."

Goal Setting: A Powerful Force

Goal setting is a very powerful force in your financial journey. If developed with thoughtfulness and regularity, goals will be one of your greatest allies. Goal development is also very forgiving. You don't have to develop "perfect" goals for them to work. Goals are like exercise. Exercise is still beneficial if you do just a little bit. Even 10 minutes a week is better than nothing. Twenty minutes is better than 10, and a half hour a day is better than both of those. An hour every day is close to optimal. Goal setting of any kind, like exercise, is beneficial. The chart below summarizes goal setting from good start to optimal. Reach for optimal, but don't get discouraged if you don't get there immediately. If you are developing any kind of financial goals, you are already way ahead of the curve!

Goal Setting Matrix: From Good to Optimal

Good Start	Informally think about goals.			
Better	Informally think about goals.	Talk about one specific goal with a partner(s). Can be short-, medium-, or long-term.		
Great	Informally think about goals.	Talk about one specific goal with a partner(s). Can be short-, medium-, or long-term.	Talk with a partner about goals. Write down all goals you talked about. Can be any combination of short-, medium-, and long-term goals. Effective method to document the conversation.	
Optimal	Informally think about goals.	Talk about one specific goal with a partner(s). Can be short-, medium-, or long-term.	Talk with a partner about goals. Write down all goals you talked about. Can be any combination of short-, medium-, and long-term goals. Effective method to document the conversation.	Systematically develop short-, medium-, and long-term goals in collaboration with a partner(s). Write down all goals and post them in a prominent place where you can see them every day. Schedule a time to revise goals on an annual or semi-annual basis.

Action Step

Write down your short-, medium-, and long-term goals and place them in a prominent place where you can see them every day.

CHAPTER 18

Increasing Your Money Knowledge

An investment in knowledge always pays the best interest.
– Benjamin Franklin

As we talked about in Chapter 17, it is very important to educate yourself about personal finance. The Japanese have a word for continuous improvement: "Kaizen." The word beautifully illustrates the concept that you should always be looking for ways to learn and improve yourself. This principle is especially true when it comes to personal finance. The ability to make adjustments and little tweaks as you gain knowledge will be invaluable as you move forward in your personal finance journey. As you no doubt have heard many people say, you are either getting better or getting worse. The following sections outline some ways to get better.

Reading Books

Some of the most successful people on the planet are and were voracious readers: Abraham Lincoln, Winston Churchill, Albert Einstein, Bill Gates, Oprah Winfrey, and Jeff Bezos are all avid readers. Warren Buffett is known to read daily for hours at a time. Oprah has her own book club she shares with audiences.[27] Reading allows you to step away from life for a set amount of time and dive deep into the material. Reading books promotes in-depth learning and high-level thinking. Books bring alive new concepts and challenges you to implement what you learn. For a moment in time, you can put away your phone, shut off your email, go to a quiet place, rid yourself of life's distractions, and engage in real learning.

Reading also opens up new doors and opportunities. Knowledge builds on itself; books frequently lead to more books and additional subject matter. For example, many books contain a page or two at the very end that include recommendations for further reading. Reading those recommended books leverages the author's experience and knowledge. This is a great shortcut. The author is telling you, "These are the books I've read to develop and increase my knowledge base—read them!" Listen to the author; he or she is giving you a shortcut to significantly increase your knowledge. In addition, certain books are almost a prerequisite to understanding more advanced books. Much like college courses have prerequisites, books can also have prerequisites.

If you read just a few high-quality books per year, you will improve your life. It's almost impossible not to. If you read several high-quality books per year, you will improve even more. In addition, the time spent reading is time *not* spent watching TV or scrolling your social media newsfeed. You ultimately get a double positive: all the inherent benefits of reading plus the subtraction of some of the time wasters we all engage in.

Articles and Blogs

Reading articles and blogs is another great way to increase your knowledge about personal finance. While not as in depth as books, articles and blogs provide a great introductory point. You can acquire new ideas, which are often timely, and many of them are simple and easy to implement. Sometimes articles and blogs take seemingly complex ideas and break them down into small, manageable pieces. "How-to" blogs are a great example of this. After reading articles or blogs, assess if you need to follow up on the subjects through books or additional research. Or if the article contained enough information, implement the strategies now. Much like books, articles and blogs can open doors to more advanced subject matter.

Articles and blogs are great substitutes for "junk food for your brain." For example, if you are waiting at the doctor or dentist's office, rather than reading a gossip magazine or scrolling through your newsfeed, pull up an article or blog on your phone about personal finance (or something else that will improve your life). This small action step will give you two wins. The first win is that you are not filling your mind with junk. The second win is that you are acquiring a small bit of knowledge that will improve your life. That article or blog you read at the dentist's office just might lead to a new idea or concept that will help you improve your life.

Podcasts

Podcasts are a relatively new way to learn information, and you can listen to them in the comfort of your car, while exercising, or just hanging around the house. The author and speaker Zig Ziglar said, "Turn your car into a rolling university." Take advantage of the time you have in your car. There are hundreds, if not thousands, of podcasts you can learn from while you're driving. Very frequently, guests on podcasts will also provide book recommendations. If you like the guest, take their book recommendations. Almost all of the books I purchase are a result of a guest recommendation from a podcast. Podcasts are also a great place to learn about additional podcasts. Many guests on podcasts also have their own shows. If you enjoyed the guest, try listening to a few episodes of their podcast. It's like when you hit it off at a party with a friend of a friend and end up hanging out with that person as much or more than your original friend.

Many of us spend an incredible amount of time in our cars. Why not take advantage of that time to learn and improve ourselves? Think of it this way: If your commute is 20 minutes to work and 20 minutes home, that's 40 minutes per day that you could be learning and acquiring new skills. Suppose that last year you worked five days a week for 47 of the 52 weeks of the year. If you listened to a podcast just during your commute times, you would have listened to 1,880 minutes of content by the end of the year! That doesn't even include other travel times like going to the store, a friend's house, or picking up the kids at practice. Even if you just listened to a podcast for half of your commute, you would have added 940 minutes of content by the end of the year. Take advantage of the time in your car; your commute is a golden opportunity to learn with minimal effort.

Audio Books

Audio books, formerly known as books on tape, are another great way to turn your car into a "rolling university." While nothing compares to sitting down to a good book, audio books are a very viable alternative, especially for long car rides. Audio books are also great for books you want to reread.

Since you've already read the book the traditional way, the audio version can act as a refresher. Additionally, many audio books are read by the author so you get to hear voice inflections as the author intended. Some authors even add a little extra to the audio versions of their book.

There are also companies that summarize entire books into less than an hour. This type of learning is great for refreshing information from a book you haven't read in a while without having to reread the entire book. Much like podcasts, audio books provide a great opportunity to increase your knowledge base in your car, on a walk, or at the gym with very minimal effort.

Clubs and Social Groups

Clubs and social groups are another great way to learn more or refine your personal finance skills. Meeting with people who have years of experience and knowledge will drive you to greater heights. They can also provide you with support, resources, and keep you focused on your financial goals. Another great thing about clubs is that they give you the opportunity to teach and mentor. Aristotle wrote, "Teaching is the highest form of mastery." Clubs and social groups provide a forum where you can be taught and teach members of the group.

Surrounding yourself with like-minded, successful people will drive you to greater heights. The more time you spend with people like this, the more you will be positively influenced. Eventually, it will be almost impossible not to acquire their habits, mindsets, and success.

Work with a Money Coach or Mentor

Working with a money coach or mentor is a great way to increase your knowledge about personal finance. The right coach will help you set goals, get more focused, and will provide education. Additionally, they will provide you with accountability and consistency on a scheduled basis. A great mentor has been there, done that. If you listen carefully and implement their advice, it can become a shortcut to success. You'll be able to avoid some of the mistakes they made. Likewise, you'll have an excellent chance to replicate some of their success.

Increasing your money knowledge comes with repetition. A good money coach will provide you with the needed structure to acquire repetition. They will set you up with weekly exercises that, if completed, will greatly expand your money knowledge and success. For example, your task one week may be to go through everything you spent money on in the past month.

Your coach will have you identify what you truly value, the necessities, and the items that really have no value at all. Those may be impulse buys or just things you thought you needed at the time. Completing this exercise will teach you more about money and your values than you thought possible. A light bulb will go off in your head, and you will gain massive clarity about what you really value and want to spend money on. This exercise alone will have a positive lasting impact on your life.

Finding the right coach or mentor is a great way to add value in your life, grow in a more focused manner, and move more quickly toward "Kaizen." There is magic and synergy in working with other people. With the help and collaboration from a money coach or mentor, you will find that you take yourself to new levels that once seemed impossible. As you work together over the days, weeks, months, and years, that growth will continue at an exponential rate that will exceed even your wildest expectations.

A good money coach will take the time to listen to you and your needs. They'll willingly answer your questions and be upfront about pricing and services. Beware of coaches who deliver high-pressure sales tactics or who bombard you with "limited time offers." Ask for referrals, and look at their track record and reviews.

Thinking Positively

One of the simplest things you can do to get better with personal finance is to think positively. It's easy to give up and resign yourself to the idea that you are not good with personal finance. There are plenty of built-in excuses, like your parents weren't good with money, your family in general isn't good with money, and you haven't had any formal education about money. Those are all excuses and need to be reframed into positive language. Instead of saying your family isn't good with money, say that you will be the first in your family to be good with money. Instead of saying you haven't had any formal education about money, say you have a great opportunity to learn about money. Excuses only hold us back; make an effort to turn excuses into positive statements. Always think positive because a positive attitude goes a long way.

Mantras

Mantras are a great way to embed positive thoughts and ideas into your head. Committing 20–30 seconds in your morning and/or evening to say a mantra will train your mind to think positive. Not just about money but about other areas of life as well. A few things you can say to yourself include:

- "I am good with money."
- "I enjoy the money process."
- "I spend my money on investments that earn me more money."
- "I am intentional with my money."
- "I understand personal finance, and there is nothing to be afraid of."
- "I am in control of my money and my life."

Rituals

Like mantras, rituals will also help you think positively every day. Many rituals have already been discussed in this book. A daily assessment of your values is a ritual. Thinking about how your spending aligns with your values is a ritual. A monthly overview with your spouse of your financial picture is another ritual. Think of rituals as an opportunity to create structure in your life that makes it impossible not to succeed. For example, if you take a brief moment every day to think about money and your life values, the concepts will become so engrained in you that your daily behaviors and spending habits will naturally start to align with your values.

Combined rituals and rituals that build on each other, are exponentially more powerful than just one ritual. For example, a daily two-minute reflection on your values and finances combined with a weekly overview of your spending, combined with a monthly overview of your larger financial picture will be significantly more powerful than doing just one of these rituals. In this example, the three rituals are interconnected and build on each other. Your thoughts lead to more intentional daily behavior, which positively impacts your weekly spending. One week of being intentional and thoughtful with your personal finances will lead to a more financially successful month, which will lead to improvement in your overall financial picture.

Taking Action

It sounds obvious, but at some point, you must take action and start doing what needs to be done. As the Nike slogan says, "Just Do It." You can learn and gather information all you want, but if you are not implementing what you have learned in real life, that learning is all for naught. There is no getting around it; the best way to learn is by doing. Books, podcasts, working with a mentor, and thinking positive are all great ways to create a knowledge base, but there is no substitute for doing.

When you go out and do it, things become real. Certain subjects or ideas you may have glossed over in a book or blog come to life when you experience them. Working through these challenges and developing creative solutions exponentially increases your learning and growth. Overcome any fear you may have and go out and do it. It may seem scary at first, but you will be glad you did. And next time it won't seem so scary. This mindset of doing things will lead to new opportunities and adventures that you otherwise would not get to experience.

Overcoming Failure and Learning From Mistakes

As you take action, you will no doubt have trials and tribulations throughout your money journey. Don't be afraid to make mistakes; they are a natural byproduct of trying new things and getting out of your comfort zone. Think of mistakes and failure as learning opportunities. Failure is part of the price you pay for success. Henry Ford said, "Those who have never made a mistake usually work for those who have."

Let's take an example of someone in her twenties who invested in a company that failed. When the company failed, she lost all the money she put into it. Initially, the failure stung, and she thought about giving up on investing. After the sting wore off, she began to analyze what happened. She realized she didn't properly vet the company and ignored many of the financial principles the company violated. She was so excited to make a quick buck that she ignored all the warning signs. Her friends also invested in the company and all they could talk about for a couple weeks was how great this company was and how much money they were going to make in just a few short months.

After a thorough review of what happened, the young investor took accountability for her financial decision and decided that although it hurt to lose her money, she would learn from this. A couple months later, a similar opportunity came up, promising quick wealth. This time she took a few days to think about it and looked at the numbers and the core values of the company. After much thought, she decided to pass. Throughout the next several decades, several similar opportunities came up, and each time she remembered the lessons from the time she lost money and carefully vetted the companies.

After several decades, the once-young investor was now a rich woman. She had passed on several losing investments her friends tried to get her into. Instead of going for the quick riches, she invested in more stable, yet slower growing assets. She found that following sound financial principles allowed her to make great financial decisions. Over the years, her investments compounded into millions of dollars. In this scenario, she learned a lesson the hard way early in life and faced failure. Rather than ignoring the failure or giving up, she became determined to learn from it and move on to smarter decisions. The lessons she learned from failure created the base for the sound financial principles she followed the rest of her life, providing her with a significant amount of money and security she wouldn't have otherwise had.

Action Steps

1. In the next four days, listen to at least one podcast pertaining to personal finance. There are some recommendations of great podcasts in Appendix B.

2. Read at least one personal finance book in the next two months, in addition to this one. See Appendix A for book recommendations.

CHAPTER 19

Spending Money to Save Money: Hiring Professionals

If you think it's expensive to hire a professional to do the job, what until you hire an amateur.
– Red Adair

Spend money to save money. It sounds like a strange concept, right? If someone is trying to save money, why would they spend more money? The reason is simple: Spending money on the right professionals can save you tremendous amounts of money and future heartache. Take the example of a small business owner. When a small business owner is establishing her company, she needs to decide how to structure the company. There are a variety of ways to legally structure a company: LLCs, sole proprietorships, partnerships, etc. Which one to pick? It's confusing, time consuming, and can ultimately cost you a lot more by making the wrong decision.

You Don't Know What You Don't Know

A small business owner can go online, read, and pick what seems to be the best option. Then she can pay a few hundred dollars and form her company online. Task complete, right? Not quite. You don't know what you don't know. This bears repeating: *You don't know what you don't know.* Unless the small business owner has an extensive knowledge base of how to structure a company, she is better served to leverage the work of a professional. A professional—an attorney in this case—will sit down with her, listen to her needs and goals, and help her pick the correct legal structure for her situation. A good, specialized attorney has probably worked with hundreds of other clients in a similar situation and can provide her with valuable and specific information pertaining to her business.

A good attorney has been there, done that, and will help you avoid future mistakes. Although it may be painful to pay more for these services upfront, it will give the small business owner a solid foundation to work from. Now imagine that same small business owner doing a little research online and paying a website a few hundred dollars to open up a sole proprietorship or LLC. That small business owner is beginning her business on a very shaky foundation that can crumble under the slightest stress or unexpected happenings. Even if the business is temporarily running successfully, without a strong foundation, the business is forever vulnerable. To reinforce the need to hire professionals, consider the following stories.

Sally and the Rental Property
Sally just purchased a rental property and needed to do some remodel work before it would be ready to rent. She met with three contractors: Ted, James, and Mary. Ted's bid came in at $14,500. He submitted a written bid and provided Sally with his contractor license and references. James said he could do the job for $7,200 but would need $5,000 upfront for materials. Mary came in at $13,750. Like Ted, Mary provided a written bid, references, and a copy of her license. Both Mary and Ted required a small deposit to pull permits.

Having just bought the rental unit, Sally was reluctant to spend much money. She was highly intrigued by James' bid. It was half the cost of the other two bids and James was nice enough. Something inside her was weary of James though. She wondered why he didn't provide a copy of his contractor's license and why he wouldn't put his bid in writing. After a few days of thinking and talking with friends, she decided to go with Mary's bid. Mary emailed her a copy of the signed contract, pulled permits within two weeks, and completed the job within a month and a half. There were no disputes, and it was quality work. Sally paid Mary and ended up using her again on two future projects. Sally has also recommended Mary to several friends and other investors.

Two years later, Mary was at a real estate meetup. One of the investors told a horror story of a contractor he had used earlier in the year. This contractor was unlicensed and ended up breaking more than he fixed. He put in the cabinets unevenly, broke a water pipe under the kitchen sink, came late or not at all most days, among other things. The real estate investor ended up having to fire this contractor and hire someone else to finish the job. All in all, this incompetent contractor ended up costing the real estate investor over $9,500. The contractor was James, who Sally had passed on. She breathed a huge sigh of relief. As the meeting ended, she quietly walked out of the meeting knowing she had made a great decision to not hire James two years earlier.

Evan and the IRS

Evan always did his taxes on his own. He thought it was simple enough: Gather documents, get the forms, and fill in the blanks. Over the past couple years, though, his taxes had been getting more challenging. Life was more complicated than when he was 18. A spouse, two kids, company dividends, and a little bit of rental income from renting out his own house on Airbnb. Evan decided to hire a CPA this year.

Evan went to CPA Maggie's office on a Thursday morning for an appointment. He brought this year's tax information along with his two previous returns, as requested. Maggie spoke with Evan and looked everything over. She explained that she could do his taxes and provided him with a written estimate of $550. Evan nearly spit out his coffee. He had always done his taxes on his own and was having trouble justifying this expense. Maggie continued, "I'm spotting some things on last year's return you might be interested in, Evan." Evan prompted her to continue. "It looks like you overpaid by $4,700."

Maggie showed Evan what she found in last year's return. Evan sheepishly looked on as Maggie identified several errors and oversights in the return. As Maggie continued to talk, Evan realized the value in hiring a professional. He couldn't believe that just two minutes ago he was actually questioning her $550 fee. She had already saved him $4,700 from last year's return and hadn't even started on this year's return. Maggie told Evan that she had all the information she needed and would have a draft of the return ready by next week.

Exactly one week later, Evan opened his email and found an encrypted draft of his tax returns from his new CPA Maggie. He was amazed at the level of organization in which Maggie prepared his returns. The returns even indicated specific tax strategies he could implement for the upcoming year to save on next year's tax returns. Evan had never thought of these strategies before and was amazed they even existed. He made the decision right then and there that Maggie would be doing his taxes from now on. This was before he got to the last page, which showed a $9,700 refund—more than the last two years combined.

The Johnson's House Hunt

The Johnson's had been in the market for a home the past six months. Mr. and Mrs. Johnson both had dutifully looked at their real estate apps to track the market in the neighborhood outside Chicago that they were interested in. They both felt confident that they knew the market well. They met with three different agents before finally deciding on Betty, a local agent with seven years of experience. Betty's professionalism and presentation during the interview made it an easy choice for the Johnsons, and she was far superior to the other two agents they had interviewed earlier in the day.

Two days later, Betty sent a group text to Mr. and Mrs. Johnson that read, "Found an off-market property that is perfect for you. Has everything you described you wanted. Another agent in my office is listing the property in two days, but I can get you in to see it this afternoon. If you like it, we can put in an offer before it is listed. Get back to me ASAP please!"

The Johnsons both met Betty at the property after work. Betty was right—they loved the house! That night, Betty wrote up an offer for $3,500 under asking price and had it submitted by 8:00 p.m. The listing agent called his client in the morning with the news. Relieved that they wouldn't have to even list the property and have people walking through the house, they immediately accepted the Johnson's offer. Just 30 days later, escrow closed and the Johnsons were officially homeowners. Mr. and Mrs. Johnson could not believe how easy Betty made the process. They were thrilled that Betty found them an off-market property, avoiding the stress of having to look at different houses and make multiple offers. Within a year, the Johnsons had recommended Betty to four of their friends. All four friends raved about what a great deal Betty found for them and how easy she made the process.

The Wednesday Night Softball League

With the emergence of the internet in the past quarter century, there is an attitude that anyone can go online, gather as much information as the professionals, and make sound decisions about any subject. Compare that to Average Joe playing in a Wednesday night softball league. Average Joe has a bat, a glove, and cleats, just like professional baseball players. The equipment is pretty much the same. Just because Average Joe has the same equipment as the pros does not mean he can play in the major leagues. Major league baseball players have a completely different skills than the average softball player. Their superior skillset comes from years of experience, practice, and natural athletic ability, among other things.

The same principle applies to Average Joe going online to research things such as tax codes, medical ailments, and legal issues. Much like the softball player, the average person does not have the skillset of a CPA, doctor, or attorney. They may have access to some information but most of the information is misunderstood or not comprehended at all. It is important to consider how much education, experience, and expertise a true professional has compared to Average Joe looking online.

High Leverage Situations

In no way should the takeaway from this chapter be that the average person can't gather information on their own. They absolutely can, and for many problems they may encounter, it makes more sense to find out information on their own. It is critical to decipher the difference between an average situation and a high-leverage situation. Many problems can be fixed by going online and watching a how-to video or reading a blog about how to do something. It might take an hour or two at most, and if you mess it up you can call someone who specializes in the issue.

Let's use yard work as an example. Suppose you have a small to medium-size yard and are debating about whether to cut the grass yourself or hire someone to do it for you. If you decide to do it yourself and mess it up, there aren't any negative long-term consequences. There isn't much risk in cutting your grass on your own. If you no longer want to do it in a month or two, you can always go out and hire someone. Once they work on your yard for a couple weeks, it will probably start to look good again.

Conversely, if you go online and try to figure out some of the high-leverage issues on your own, there is a lot to risk. In the example about Evan and the CPA, Evan performed a high-leverage situation on his own and lost out on a lot of money over the years. He didn't even realize some of the errors he made because he didn't know enough. It's the same with the small business owner who tries to create a company online. She is putting the business at risk before it even starts because the legal struc-ture of the company was likely not done correctly. Both of these examples are high-leverage situations that if not done correctly, may end up costing someone a lot of money, put them at legal risk, or a combination of both.

The higher-leverage the situation is, the more important it is to hire a professional. Your role is to determine what is high-leverage and what tasks can be performed with minimal risk. You also need to be aware of and clearly assess your own limits. Some questions to ask yourself that will help you in this determination:

- What am I trying to accomplish?
- How much knowledge of the subject do I have?
- Are most people in my industry hiring this out?
- Are people in my peer group hiring this out?
- What is the risk versus reward?
- Are there things I don't know about performing this task?
- Are there legal ramifications for getting this wrong?
- What are the financial consequences?
- Is this work normally performed by a licensed professional, some-one with an advanced degree, or a combination of both? Example: doctor, lawyer, CPA
- Is it possible that I don't know what I don't know?
- If carefully thought out and honestly answered, your answers to these questions will guide you on what you should do.

Leverage the Experience of Others

Hiring professionals allows you to leverage someone else's expertise and experience. It keeps you from learning from the "school of hard knocks" and making costly mistakes. Professionals know and have seen things that you have not. They know the pitfalls and can help navigate you to the most cost-efficient choices. They save you money and keep you out of trouble. Think of it like this: You are paying a set amount of money for a professional to use all the knowledge and training they have on your particular problem or situation. You are leveraging thousands of their hours of experience and years of training and school on your problem. What do you get when you hire a professional? See the chart below for the years of training and certifications needed for each profession.

Profession	Combined Years of School and Training	Required to Pass State Boards?
CPA	16+	Yes
Dentist	20+	Yes
Doctor	23+	Yes
Lawyer	19+	Yes

True professionals have years and years of education and experience. Paying for that experience and level of expertise is the smart and prudent thing to do. There's an old parable that illustrates this point: the parable about the repairman and the hammer has been told in different ways throughout the years but it goes something like this.:

A very expensive machine that is essential to the factory breaks down one day. This machine has to be working for the factory to produce anything. The supervisor of the factory calls in a repairman who comes in to inspect and repair the machine. Upon walking into the factory, the repairman walks around the machine, takes a look, and pulls out his hammer. He taps the machine, and voila! The machine starts working good as new. The repairman tells the supervisor that will be $500. The supervisor is furious at the price, exclaiming that all he did was tap the machine a few times. The supervisor proceeds to demand an itemized bill. The next day the repairman walks back into the factory with an itemized bill. It reads:

1. Tapping the machine with a hammer: $1
2. Knowing where to tap the machine: $499

So the next time you need to hire someone, think about the story of the repairman and the hammer. Have you been struggling with something that a professional could figure out quickly? Are you wasting time in an area where you have no knowledge? Think about whether it would save you time and money to hire someone else to do it.

Don't Think of It as Help

A lot of us don't like to ask for help. We feel like we should be doing and figuring everything out ourselves. We think asking for help is a sign of weakness and possibly incompetence. Adjust your mindset to think of asking for help as leveraging the experience of others. Leveraging the experience of others is anything but a sign of weakness. It's actually a sign of great strength. It's a sign that you have the wisdom to understand there are certain tasks you should do and shouldn't do. For the ones you shouldn't do, rely on the experience of highly qualified people. You will find that your life becomes easier and you'll get more done, have more time with your family, and rest easier at night knowing you picked the right person.

Action Step

Pick one high-leverage area of your life where it would save you time and money to hire a professional, rather than do it yourself. Hire that professional the next time you need their services–and make sure to ask friends and associates for recommendations before hiring them.

CHAPTER 20

Highest and Best Use of Time

The word "no" is a great time saver. Say no to anything that is not the highest and best use of your time.
– Brian Tracy

An element of your financial journey is discovering your highest and best use of time. All too often people try to save money by taking on DIY, or do it yourself, projects that end in frustration and copious amounts of time spent. Think carefully about what you do best. This has a direct relationship to your highest and best use of time. How much is your time worth by the hour? How much do you enjoy doing particular projects?

Calculating Your Time

Take, for example, a real estate agent, small business owner, or someone in a commission-based occupation. If the real estate agent can average one sale per every four open houses they hold on a weekend, they may want to think twice about spending several hours on the weekends doing household chores or yardwork. A real estate agent in this situation would want to carefully analyze exactly how many hours it takes to close one transaction for every four open houses they hold. He or she should calculate the time spent advertising for the open house, putting out signs, setting up, holding the open house, cleaning up, writing offers, and negotiating the final price. He or she would then assign a dollar value per hour on his or her time. This will help determine highest and best use of time versus doing household chores, yardwork, and other DIY projects they don't enjoy. The chart below illustrates this point.

Time Cost Example (Real Estate Agent)

	Time Cost	Multiplied by four (four open houses)
Advertising	0.5 hours	2 hours
Talking with neighbors	1.5 hours	6 hours
Putting out and picking up signs	0.5 hours	2 hours
Set up and clean up	0.5 hours	2 hours
Holding house open	3 hours	12 hours
Writing offers	1.5 hours	N/A
Negotiation	4 hours	N/A
Inspections	3 hours	N/A
Miscellaneous paperwork and tasks	3 hours	N/A
Travel Time	1 hour	4 hours
Total Time	18.5 hours	28 hours

Average commission earned for every four open houses held on the weekend (after taxes)	$2,700
Average dollar amount earned per hour	$96

A real estate agent with these statistics would determine that their highest and best use of time is $96 per hour. Any kind of DIY project that does not exceed $96 per hour is not an optimal use of their time. For example, suppose the agent in the example has a landscaping project where he or she has to dig for irrigation, install sprinklers, level the yard, and more. The project is expected to take 25 hours and will save approximately $1,900. The real estate agent in this project is "paying" himself approximately $76 per hour, compared to the $96 per hour that he would earn selling a home. If the agent does not enjoy this type of work and is not good at it, he would be much better off working to sell a home. It's not only more money but also something the agent enjoys and is good at. This concept does not factor in other variables that will be addressed later such as doing projects you enjoy and spending time on projects with family.

It's Not Just for Commission-Based Jobs

Factoring in the most profitable and best use of time isn't just limited to commission-based occupations. It also applies to jobs where overtime can be earned, such as a police officer, a fire fighter, or a nurse. Much like the formula with the real estate agent, anyone in an occupation for overtime potential should carefully analyze their highest and best use of time. For example, if a nurse can earn $75 an hour for overtime, the highest and best use of his time in a dollar amount is $75 an hour. That's assuming that overtime is relatively easy to get and the tasks fall within the normal scope of the job. If the nurse in this example works an eight-hour overtime shift on a Saturday, he will earn an additional $600.

If there's a DIY project at home he does not particularly want to do, or is unskilled at, he needs to weigh the cost of completing the DIY project to his highest and best hourly wage. For example, if there is a semi-major plumbing issue that would cost $900 to pay someone to do, the nurse in our example would need to calculate the time it would take him to complete the project and break it down to an hourly rate. The nurse in our example calculated the following:

Activity	Estimated Time Amount
Research project	3 hours
Purchase supplies	1.5 hours
Set up	1.5 hours
Perform activity	7 hours
Back and forth trips to hardware store mid-project	2 hours
Test and clean up	2 hours
Total	17 hours
Total Money Saved	$53 hour, $900 for the project

In this example, the DIY project would take the nurse approximately 17 hours to complete in order to save $900, or $53 per hour. 17 hours of overtime equates to $1,275, or $75 per hour. The highest and best use of time in this example is clearly to work the overtime. The most obvious advantages to working the overtime are:

1. The overtime is in an area the nurse has expertise in, enjoys, and is good at.
2. The overtime is more of a known entity whereas myriad problems are likely to arise in a DIY plumbing project for a person with a low skill level. I can certainly attest to this, such as when my plumbing "project" turned into a waterfall cleanup project. The quintessential "Pandora's Box" is opened in any type of project like this.

You Don't Always Have to Do It Yourself or Work Extra

The strategies and examples above are intended to present another way of thinking about the value of your time. It does not mean that every time a project comes up, you have to either do it yourself or work extra at your job to pay for it. One of the beauties of embedding emergency savings into your monthly bills is that you can avoid making these decisions entirely. If you have savings for emergencies, you can always just pay directly from that account to fund projects. The point of this section is simply to carefully analyze whether you want to be completing DIY projects and to provide you with alternatives. As long as you have emergency savings embedded into your monthly savings, you can have the best of both worlds—you can have the option of paying someone to complete a project and literally have it be done when you return from taking the kids to the zoo.

When Should You Complete DIY Projects?

DIY projects should *only* be taken on if at least one of the following conditions are met:

1. You have some skill level in the area.
2. You enjoy the project and want to spend time doing it.
3. Appropriate cost savings: the cost to do it yourself is enough of a savings that it's worth your time and effort to do it yourself.
4. You have a friend skilled in the area who can help you.
5. You consciously want to perform the project with family members.

You Have Some Skill Level in the Area

If you have some skill level in an area, it may be worth your time to take on a DIY project. However, you need to have at least a basic skill level, preferably a high skill level. For example, if you have been working on cars your whole life and understand how to do a lot more than change the oil, it is probably worth your time to work on cars. If a mechanic charges $1,000 in labor to change the timing belt and you can do it yourself in five hours, that's a savings of $1,000 for five hours of work. That comes out to $200 an hour for your time and efforts. If you are skilled in this area, it probably makes sense to do your own car repairs. Over time, that can save a tremendous amount of money.

You Enjoy the Project and Want to Spend Time Doing It

Many people enjoy certain DIY projects. Gardening is a great example of this. Many people enjoy spending time outdoors and getting their hands dirty. They enjoy the sunshine, watching the birds, and chatting with the neighbors while doing the actual gardening. Gardening is something they love to do and would do it even if it didn't come with any cost benefit. If there are projects around the house you absolutely love to do or even mildly enjoy, you probably want to keep doing those activities on a regular basis.

Others love working on boats, cars, trucks, go-karts, or anything with an engine. People like that should absolutely take on DIY projects with anything mechanical. It's also a great opportunity to involve the kids and spend time together on projects. Additionally, it's a good way to teach your children some valuable skills that may even become a future career. These are great DIY projects because they are enjoyable and do not feel like work at all. They are a good way to relax and engage in an enjoyable activity.

Appropriate Cost Savings

In some projects, the cost to do it yourself is significant enough that it's worth your time and effort. You will also want to have some level of skill in performing the task. As an example, I recently had a few shrubs that needed to be pulled out of my front yard. It would have cost $300–$400 to hire someone to do the work. I estimated it would take me about two hours to pull them out myself and clean up. I estimated that to be $150–$200 per hour for my time so I chose to do it myself. The project didn't involve plumbing or electrical, so I felt comfortable doing it myself even though it wasn't exactly fun. And $150–$200 per hour for yardwork was worth the time and effort for me in that situation.

Other examples of DIY work that can provide enough of a cost savings to make it worthwhile include painting the interior of a home, power washing the driveway, putting together furniture, and deep cleaning a small home. Everyone has their list of things they are able to do and list of things they are not willing or skilled enough to do. Think about your list and act accordingly.

Skilled Friend

All of us have that friend who seemingly can do any kind of handy work. If your friend is willing to help (by help, I mean take the lead on the project while you hand them the beverage of their choice) and provide you with a significant cost savings, you may want to take them up on their offer. Especially if you can repay them by trading a skill you have for their work. For example, if you are a CPA, maybe you can trade doing their taxes for their help on the backyard fence. Or maybe the trade is simply a 30-pack and a thank you in exchange for their help. Getting help from friends can save a significant amount of money while getting skilled help from a trustworthy person.

Completion with Family

There may be some DIY projects you specifically want to perform with family members. For example, a DIY project that you want to teach your daughter and/or son. The motive isn't necessarily to complete the project but to teach your child the value of working on something all the way to completion. Maybe you want to teach your child how to cut the grass, trim the shrubs, and pick the weeds. Perhaps, you want to show the value of hard work and what it takes to get things done—to let them know these things require work, or finding a way to pay someone else. You may have no intention of teaching this as a vocation but simply want to provide your child with life lessons.

Others may want to work with their children/family on DIY projects as a way to bond and spend time together. There is a certain satisfaction in getting a job done and even more satisfaction in doing it together as family. Working on cars, boats, go-carts, etc. are a favorite pastime for many families. Everyone works together and hangs out at the same time. These are great opportunities for life lessons and bonding.

Action Step

Identify your highest and best use of time and live accordingly.

CHAPTER 21

Financial Independence

Financial independence is the ability to live from the income of your own personal resources.

– Jim Rohn

Financial independence, or financial freedom, is when your passive income stream exceeds your monthly expenses, creating a positive monthly cash flow. For many years, this has been called retirement. Work most of your life, then enjoy your golden years without having to worry about money—that's traditional retirement. However, things are evolving and changing, and a growing number of people are no longer satisfied with the traditional retirement model of working until age 65. Applying even some of the financial principles from this book will quicken the process towards financial freedom.

The earlier financial independence is earned, the less time you are required to work for money. Notice the language here—*required*. Many people choose to continue to work, but it's because they love what they do and it's no longer about having to work just to pay the monthly bills. People in this situation are working for purpose, fun, or other personal reasons. They are not required to work for money, which makes all the difference in the kind of work they are willing to perform. Those in this position are very selective about their time. What would you do with your time if you didn't have to work for money anymore?

It's All About the Monthly Cash Flow

It's easy to go through money quickly. And when it's gone, it's gone. The key to financial freedom is sustainable cash flow on a monthly basis. It's much harder to go through monthly cash flow if you do two things:

1. Determine how much you need monthly, along with how much you likely will need as you age.

2. Create the appropriate amount of passive cash flow to support your monthly living standard. Remember to include everything in your monthly living standard. This includes food, shelter, entertainment, cushion money for miscellaneous items, emergencies, long-term care (towards later years), etc. Once your monthly passive cash flow exceeds your expenses, you are financially free. For extra financial security, overshoot your estimate by 10 percent or more to account for any errors or highly unexpected occurrences.

There are a few keys here. The first is the word "passive." The monthly cash flow has to be passive for you to be truly financially free. That means you don't have to work for money. This is one of the biggest errors people make in their calculations. They include income from employment or business in addition to passive income in their monthly cash flow calculations. It is fine to include all sources of income, just realize you are still having to work for money if including employment. To be truly financially free, the monthly calculation has to be passive income only. There will come a time in everyone's life where they either don't want to work for money anymore or are unable to work for money anymore. It's important to realize this and plan for that time.

As an example, Natasha has a monthly pension she receives from her years of employment. Her pension creates a passive income stream that covers almost all of her monthly bills. This includes vacations, savings, daily living, etc. However, Natasha also works a part-time job up to 20 hours per week. She has gotten into the habit of buying what she wants and just working extra when she needs the money. This has worked for Natasha for many years without a hitch. However, when Natasha is no longer wanting to or able to work her part-time job, she will be cash flow negative. She believes she is financially free but continues to work for money every time she buys something or goes on a vacation. This strategy has been successful over the years, but there will come a time when it won't work. The best course of action for Natasha is to increase her passive stream of income so that everything is covered. This probably will mean continuing her part-time work and investing a large portion of the money to create additional passive cash flow.

Increasing Monthly Cash Flow

A great way to increase monthly cash flow is to put more earned income into investments. In Natasha's case, she is in the habit of working more when she has bills to pay. Go on vacation more, work more. Buy a new couch, work more. This is not financial freedom. To become truly financially free, Natasha needs to be able to cover all her expenses, including vacations and items she routinely purchases each month, using just passive income.

The old plan had Natasha going on vacation and working extra to cover any additional bills. The revised plan has Natasha working to cover the extra vacation bill but also contributing more to her investments at the same time. Continuing to use Natasha as an example, suppose a vacation she wants to take costs $3,700. Natasha is able to cover $2,900 of that cost via her passive income stream, leaving her $800 short. She then works just enough hours to make up the $800. In the new strategy, Natasha will work additional hours and contribute excess funds into an investment strategy of her choice: let's use $500 as a nice round number.

The new scenario looks like this: She works enough to cover the $800 deficit and enough to pay her investment $500. For the purposes of this example, suppose that Natasha owns an investment property. The remaining principle and interest is $21,000, with a monthly payment of $625. Natasha can chip away at the balance by working extra at her part-time job. When the property is paid off, she has an additional $625 per month of added passive income. This added income will help fill in the gaps for trips and nonnecessities. So instead of being $800 short like she was in the previous vacation example, Natasha is now only $175 ($800 minus $625) short for the vacation. She now has the option of working more to fill in the gap or going on a slightly less expensive vacation and not working extra at all. After she pays off her investment property using this strategy, she will be very close to financial independence.

Think Passive Income

Always be thinking about passive income. Create a mindset for yourself that passive income will pay for your life and create financial freedom. Always be on the lookout for opportunities to increase passive income. Whether that's contributing extra money to a particular investment, finding a great real estate deal, or paying down an asset, always look to increase passive income. This principle will guide you to a life of abundance and opportunity. Go back to your goals and see if you have listed increasing passive income as an entry. If it's listed, great. If not, create a goal to increase your passive income. To be truly financially free, every month needs to be cash flow positive. Be honest with yourself about your expenses in your assessment, this is not the time to "fudge" the numbers because it will come back to bite you later. Create a passive income stream that easily covers your monthly expenses.

To use another example, if Bill is cash flow positive eight out of 12 months with just his passive income, but has four months where he owes an average of $750 a month, he is not yet financially free. Bill needs to fill in the gaps to eliminate the four months of expenses. Bill may be able to get away with the cash flow negative months for a year or two but over time it will catch up to him. Bill doesn't want to get himself into a situation where he has to go back to work when he's older or unable to work, so it's in his best interest to fill in the gaps now while he is still working.

To reiterate, it is essential to be honest with yourself during this process. It is human nature to manipulate the numbers to make yourself feel better. If you tinker with the numbers to give the illusion of financial freedom, it will only hurt you in the end. Be honest with yourself and create a real plan so that you truly are financially free and never have to worry about working for money again. You'll still have the option to continue working but you will no longer need to work.

Two Approaches

As you journey toward financial freedom, there are a couple simple strategies to increase monthly income. It can come in the form of increasing monthly cash flow via making more money in work or investments or it can come in the form of eliminating expenses, thus increasing monthly income. Both approaches work. Even more powerful would be to implement a hybrid approach, combining both strategies to create a higher monthly income stream. As an example, if John gets a raise of $200 per month and cuts his monthly expenses by $100, he just created $300 in net increased income. Let's talk about a few different ways John can use this money to increase his future income stream.

John can put $200 toward his investments, which will pay off later in the form of monthly passive income. In this case, suppose he puts the money into an index fund. The remaining $100 can go toward the debt payoff of his rental property. Both of the "buckets" John is putting his money into will create a passive stream of income later in life. Or John can put all $300 into an index fund and not contribute anything extra to the rental property. Or John can put all $300 into the rental property pay down and nothing into the index fund. The idea is to execute strategies that will increase monthly cash flow. How it's done is up to the individual, which is one of the beauties of personal finance. There are endless ways to win; you get to pick what works for you.

Endless Opportunities and the Ability to Choose

Aligning your spending with your values has the potential to greatly speed up the journey toward financial independence. Instead of money being wasted on things you don't really want or value, money is invested in assets. Assets produce income, and when you have lots of assets, there is a great amount of income generated. This creates a passive income stream that can sustain an individual over a lifetime, leaving the individual with the ability to not have to work for money any longer. Planning, aligning your spending with your values, and staying true to the plan will yield extraordinary results. When you no longer are required to work for money, endless opportunities await.

Reaching financial independence gives you the ability to choose: You can choose where you want to work, what you want to do, or even if you want to work at all. Or a combination of all of the above; maybe you want to work seven months out of the year and travel the remaining five. Or do some freelance work while you travel. When your monthly passive income exceeds your monthly bills, the choices you make are no longer driven by financial constraints. This gives you an increased power in your life. You are exponentially freer to make life decisions without having to worry much about money. What would your life look like with these kinds of choices?

Much of the stress in today's world stems from the combination of work and finances and everything that comes with it. Most people work because they have to pay the bills and keep the family afloat. They live paycheck to paycheck and work long hours. Unfortunately, some people even stay in jobs they hate because they need to pay the bills. Financial independence gives us more freedom. If you are financially independent, you do not have to deal with traffic every morning or with a boss you don't like. You provide yourself with increased control in your daily and long-term future. That is very powerful. If you are no longer in a position where you need to work for money, you are much more likely to find employment you really like or adjust the terms of your current career to increase enjoyment.

Increased Opportunities

Being financially independent provides you with increased opportunities, not only in life but also in business. If you are no longer relying on a month-to-month paycheck, you'll be able to take more financial and business risks. That may mean starting your own company or taking on another type of entrepreneurial endeavor. You can do something you love or that you are especially good at. Since you're not relying on a consistent paycheck, there is a margin for error if the business endeavor does not make money immediately. You can still pay the bills with your passive income. In no way am I encouraging you to go years without profit or growth, or any hope of growth. What it does allow for is more organic growth at a rate you are comfortable with. Abraham Lincoln said that if he had six hours to chop down a tree, he would spend the first four hours sharpening the axe. Without needing immediate profit, you can take the time to "sharpen the saw" by spending more time on planning and development of your business idea.

Over time, as a business owner develops his or her company, there are endless opportunities for a much higher income. The business may start slow during the development phases but it will grow at an exponential rate as systems are carefully put into place. Time and control are on the side of a financially free entrepreneur.

Following Her Dreams

Consider the story of Gina. She is 42 years old with two kids, a husband, one dog, and five goldfish. She and her husband began investing in index funds immediately after college. The family has a sizeable portfolio and is at the point where neither of them need to work for money any longer. Gina's husband enjoys his job as a fireman and has no desire to retire or reduce his hours anytime soon. Gina, however, grew tired of her high-paying corporate job so she decided to leave last year and start her own company. Since the family invested wisely in index funds, they no longer rely on her high salary. She is free to take a risk to do something she really enjoys.

Ever since she was a small child, Gina has always loved playing basketball. She is also a very savvy businessperson. She had been thinking for some time that she could combine her love of basketball with her business skills. In addition, Gina wanted to give back to the community that had given so much to her as a child. An idea popped into her head: Why not start a basketball coaching program for at-risk youth? She could leverage her business skills with her love of basketball and desire to give back. It was the perfect idea for her. As soon as Gina left her corporate job, she went to work for herself.

Gina started slowly by getting the word out to some local high schools that she was looking for student volunteers. She also reached out to several of her business contacts for donations. After a year, Gina had a staff of three high school kids along with several thousand dollars in donations. That summer, Gina ran one-week basketball camps from June until late August. Hundreds of kids from the local community attended during the summer. Gina got to coach basketball and make a difference, like so many coaches had done for her years ago. During the next several years, her nonprofit grew from summer camps to also include weekend and after school basketball clinics. Gina's basketball clinics were open almost every day out of the year, making a huge difference in the lives of kids who really needed it. She was loving what she was doing and was even taking a small salary as the CEO of her nonprofit. Gina had never been happier and was thankful that she made the decision to leave her high paying corporate job for something she loved.

Hobby Business

Many financially independent people simply choose to create a hobby business. For example, somebody who really enjoys woodworking could create a small woodworking business out of his garage and only sell to certain vendors or friends or family. Orders could be taken weeks or even months out because an immediate profit is not needed. The owner of a hobby business may take three to four weeks of vacation, work a week or two, then go on another trip before completing a project. In a hobby business, extra money is generated but it is not a necessity. This type of business also avoids pressure from customers.

Small Startups

Another option is to join a small startup with large growth potential. A financially independent person can afford to go through some lean years while the business is getting off the ground. He or she will also have the potential to work closely with the CEO during the beginning stages, creating opportunity for future responsibility as desired. This might be an opportunity for someone who does not want to start their own company but who wants to be involved with something from the ground up.

Increased Ability to Help Others

There are endless ways to help others through your knowledge of personal finance. As you make progress toward personal finance mastery, you will probably have a desire to help others. It feels great to help others, and it is very powerful to know that you are making a big difference in the lives of one or many. Helping others does not necessarily involve donating or giving money to others, although that is a powerful medium. There are many ways to help others.

Mentoring

You've read the books, attended the courses, done the research, learned through trial and error, and implemented everything into practice. You've learned a lot through the years. Your knowledge has made a life-changing difference for you and your family, and now you want to pass it along to others. Mentoring is a great way to pass on your knowledge. There are a variety of ways to provide mentorship. It can be as simple as going out to coffee with someone on a semi-regular basis to talk personal finance. Or it can be on a more intense level where you are working directly with them to create systems or act as an accountability partner. Mentoring can be as much or as little as you and your mentee desire, and much of it will evolve and grow organically over time. Come in with a mindset to help and let the relationships grow.

Mentoring can also simply come from being a positive role model and leading by example. Others will invariably notice and observe your success in personal finances. They are going to notice your relaxed demeanor, the time you spend with your family, your ability to always be at your kids sporting events, among other things. When others are talking negatively about money, people will notice that you never have a negative thing to say. Instead, you'll be talking about personal accountability, focusing only on what you can control, and being focused. People will take notice and seek wisdom from you.

Donations and Work with Charities

There are literally thousands of charities out there. Pick one or start one yourself. Having control of your personal finances provides you with the tremendous gift of being able to help others both financially and with the gift of time. Go back to your values again. What do you value and who do you want to help? Who and what do you believe in? The answers to these questions will guide you to the right charity. You are in control, give the time and money that feels right to you.

Private Money

For many, giving to charity isn't personal enough so they find people on their own to help. Maybe your gardener brings his teenage son to work with him every weekend. The son never complains, works hard, and is respectful. He's told you on a few occasions that has good grades but is worried about being able to afford college. You might decide that you want to help this kid through college. Or give the family a substantial Christmas bonus. Maybe the Uber driver that took you to the airport was extra helpful and cheerful so you want to give her a $100 tip. The beauty of it is that you get to decide.

Before Financial Independence

Once you write down your financial goals and develop a plan to reach them, a huge weight will be lifted off your shoulders. You will go from not having a plan to a tangible way to reach all your financial goals. All that you need to do now is implement the plan over time. As the years pass, you will start to feel less pressure at work and life in general. You will have more options. We all see it every day: People rushing around, speeding, and in a panic to get to work or an appointment. Having a clear plan towards reaching financial independence will eliminate a lot of that rushing around because your financial life is under control. When your financial life is under control, other parts of life seem to follow. Making progress towards financial independence will give you an everyday sense of control and power over your professional and personal life. It is amazing what a simple plan and subsequent action steps can do to reduce daily stress levels.

When it comes to creating your personal finance plan, the earlier the better. As soon as you can develop, plan, and take action, the better off you will be. Imagine the difference between someone who starts their journey at age 23 versus age 53. That's 30 years of time that could have been spent with a clear plan and execution—30 more years of purposeful and meaningful execution. Those who get started investing early are able to make exponentially more in returns versus those who get started later. If you are reading this and are getting started late, don't be discouraged. Remember, if you haven't already started the planning, the best time to do it is today. As a Chinese proverb says, "The best time to plant a tree was 20 years ago. The second best time is now."

In your journey to financial independence, make sure to stop and smell the roses. It is easy to get hyper-focused on the goal while forgetting to enjoy life. Find the right balance for yourself—you can move quickly toward your goal, help others, and enjoy life to the fullest all at the same time. They are not mutually exclusive and should not be treated as such. Take the time to enjoy life and remember with the right planning and follow through, financial independence will come.

Action Step

Take a minute to write down how you would live your life differently if you no longer had to work for money.

Final Thoughts

For your own success to be real, it must contribute to the success of others.
— Eleanor Roosevelt

Working toward financial freedom is a process of learning, growing, and taking action. Many of the principles in this book involve a new way of thinking. The concepts are not complicated; they are fairly obvious when broken down and dissected. Identify what you value and let your values drive your spending. Use common sense. Avoid impulse buys. Don't try and keep up with the Joneses. Pay yourself first. These are all relatively simple principles, but they require awareness and action to implement.

We live in a culture of spending. Advertisers are all trying to get you to spend, spend, spend. Friends and family seem to spend endlessly. It takes discipline and intentionality to behave differently than those around us. And it's not easy to do. It takes a change in behavior and moving away from the crowd to invest in assets, rather than just buying "stuff." Friends and family will question you on what you're doing. Coworkers will question you. People may not understand what you are doing because they have never thought the way you do.

Don't worry though; it really doesn't matter what others think of you. What matters is the progress you make toward the goals you set for yourself and your family. As you begin to reach your goals, your confidence will greatly increase. Every goal you reach will be a victory. Your many victories will build on each other, creating even greater victories. The victories will come in abundance, and your financial situation will also grow in abundance. It will almost become easy.

However, it takes work to get to the easy stage. Reading this book is a great start but without taking action, it's just information and entertainment. Derek Sivers says, "If more information was the answer, then we'd all be billionaires with perfect abs."[28] You have to get the ball rolling, start gathering momentum, and take action. It's possible that you won't even recognize the progress at first. But over the course of weeks, months, years, and decades, those small actions will really add up. After only a few years, your financial situation will become almost unrecognizable compared to where you are today. So start making the changes today and keep at it. You can do it.

---

28   Tim Ferriss, "Tools of Titans Distilled (#202)," *The Tim Ferris Show*, (November 21, 2016), https://tim.blog/2016/11/21/tools-of-titans-derek-sivers-distilled/.

Appendix A: Book Recommendations

Personal Finance

David Bach, *The Automatic Millionaire*

David Bach, *The Latte Factor*

George S. Clason, *The Richest Man in Babylon*

J. L. Collins, *The Simple Path to Wealth*

Robert T. Kiyosaki, *Rich Dad's Cashflow Quadrant*

Robert T. Kiyosaki, *Rich Dad's Retire Rich, Retire Young*

Robert T. Kiyosaki, *Rich Dad, Poor Dad*

Dave Ramsey, *Total Money Makeover*

Vicki Robin, *Your Money or Your Life*

Thomas J. Stanley and William D. Danko, *The Millionaire Next Door*

Scott Trench, *Set for Life*

Real Estate

David Greene, *Long-Distance Real Estate Investing*

Gary Keller, *The Millionaire Real Estate Investor*

Brandon Turner, *The Book on Rental Property Investing*

Non-Finance Books

David Allen, *Getting Things Done*

James Allen, *As A Man Thinketh*

Bob Burg and John David Mann, *The Go-Giver*

Dale Carnegie, *How to Win Friends and Influence People*

James Clear, *Atomic Habits*

Paulo Coelho, *The Alchemist*

Stephen R. Covey, *The 7 Habits of Highly Effective People*

Charles Duhigg, *The Power of Habit*

Angela Duckworth, *Grit*

Annie Duke, *Thinking in Bets*

Hal Elrod, *Miracle Morning*

Darren Hardy, *The Compound Effect*

Napoleon Hill, *Think and Grow Rich*

Spencer Johnson, *Who Moved My Cheese?*

Gary Keller, *The One Thing*

Jim Loehr and Tony Schwartz, *The Power of Full Engagement*

Og Mandino, *The Greatest Salesman in the World*

Jim Rohn, *The Twelve Pillars*

David J. Schwartz, *The Magic of Thinking Big*

Robin Sharma, *The Monk Who Sold His Ferrari*

Chris Voss, *Never Split the Difference*

Bill Walsh, *The Score Takes Care of Itself*

Jocko Willink and Leif Babin, *Extreme Ownership*

John Wooden, *Wooden on Leadership*

Appendix B: Podcast Recommendations

Bigger Pockets Business Podcast

Bigger Pockets Money Podcast

Bigger Pockets Real Estate Podcast

The Brian Buffini Show

DarrenDaily on Demand

Choose FI

The David Bach Show

Dough Roller

The Real Estate Guys

Success Habits of Super Achievers

Appendix C: Personal Finance Website Recommendations

https://affordanything.com/

https://biggerpockets.com/

https://www.choosefi.com/

https://www.coachcarson.com/

https://davidbach.com/

https://www.doughroller.net/

https://financialmentor.com/

https://financialpanther.com/

https://www.getrichslowly.org/

https://jlcollinsnh.com/

https://www.madfientist.com/

https://millennialmoney.com/

https://www.makingsenseofcents.com/

https://www.millionaireeducator.com/

https://www.mrmoneymustache.com/

https://ptmoney.com/

https://www.stackingbenjamins.com/

Acknowledgments

This book was a team effort. There's no way I could have finished it without the help and encouragement of so many great people.

Thank you to my mom, dad, and sister for all their love and support over the years. You've always believed in me and that means a lot.

To my wife, Jennifer, you're the best. You inspire me every day and pushed me to finish this book. Your belief that I would make this book a success means the world to me.

To my two daughters, I'll always remember the 5:00 a.m. writing sessions when you'd wake up and lay next to me on the couch while I wrote. Your smiles and energy light up my world every day. This book is for the two of you.

Thank you to my mother and father-in-law for all the love and support you give our family.

To my great friends, there are too many to name, thank you.

Thank you to the incredibly talented people at Book Launchers who worked on this book. Your edits and incredible feedback made all the difference.

About the Author

Aaron Nannini is the founder of cashuncomplicated.com. When he's not writing about personal finance, Aaron loves spending time with his wife, two daughters, and German Shepherd. An avid traveler, he has been to all 50 states and has visited countries throughout Europe, Africa, and North America. To share your success stories and to inquire about speaking engagements, please visit his website at cashuncomplicated.com.

CPSIA information can be obtained
at www.ICGtesting.com
Printed in the USA
LVHW050413080221
678682LV00014B/1059